FOR GOD'S SAKE

FOR GOD'S SAKE

by

Norma E. Leary

ABOUT THE BOOK

For God's Sake, is a collection off squibs and thought provoking ideas *for* readers hoping to revive lost amenities and get them in action again for the sake of God and our national sanity.

Peppered with nostalgia, humor, admonitions and "around the corner suggestions, *For God's Sake* will leave you cheering or with your dander up. Maybe both.

The gradual demise of good manners, pleasing dress, correct grammar, modern conveniences that are more of a hindrance than a help, *are* a few topics writer Norma Leary takes to task. Also, under the gun is the rampant apathy that's turning us into lazy, immoral zombies.

Scattered throughout the text are random bits fashioned to give readers a breather from the deluge of opinionated musings. These include some games and stunts for children to enjoy and cartoons eminating from Leary's work as a church organist. The book's format is ideal for reading in starts and stops, a help for those rushing about trying to keep body and soul together.

The author's intent is to urge us to either arouse our comatose courtesies or become more fearful, lonely and disgusted than we are. The premise of, *For God's Sake*, is that times are hectic but not hopeless if good people will get up and going.

Prelude

Johann Sebastian Bach said There's nothing to it. Just hit the right note at the right time and the instrument plays itself."

"Music washes away from the soul the dust of everyday life. The best music is what it should be, sacred. The highest graces of music flow from feelings of the heart." (anonymous)

"Hug the musicians--they never get to dance." (Marilyn Campbell)

I remember hearing Grandmother despairing, "What's the world coming to? I do declare, we're going to hell in a handbasket 2'

She often exchanged "handbasket" for "broom stick" and a few times expressed worry that neither conveyance was roomy enough to hold all those deserving of the ride. No, she wasn't more self-righteous or judgmental than the rest of us, just worried about the gradual loss of the social mores designed to make life more civil, safe and pleasant.

Lamenting that progress was progressing faster than she could keep up, she took exception to, "Times are changing", exclaiming, "Well, land of Goshen, why do people have to change with the times?"

Later, as mother grew older, she parroted the same concerns as had her mother. Their frettings gave me the unsettling feelings that I, and my generation, were to blame for this "pretty kettle of fish". It didn't occur to them that their generations were responsible. Nor did they willingly bow to the inevitability of change being more difficult to deal with as one ages.

I vowed I'd never stoop to such railings. I'm older now and I have. Reminds me of mother saying, "Just wait. One day you'll wish you could set the clock back." She also explained that I became her sounding board because so many of her friends had died and she had few left with whom to chat or commiserate about the "good old days".

Well, I've arrived, feet first, in stewing about the niceties we, as a society, have abandoned. Not an exponent of "silence is golden" when voices beg to be heard, I truly believe it's time to speak up on the side of the valuable values we yell about being lost but have failed to define for our younger people. Since reform from the top down has never worked, our only salvation is for youth and young parents to seriously consider that advantage of reinstating the amenities meant to keep us sane. This won't happen unless and until we explain what it is that's missing.

Good manners, for instance, stem from being thoughtful, being thoughtful is being kind, being kind is being loving and being loving is being what God has in mind for us. Good manners extend to paying bills on time, living within or below your income, being a good steward of your belongings and not wasting anything, time included. (Let me tell you, when you get older and time is running out, to "kill" time is a sin.)

Keeping promises, dressing for the occasion, keeping a neat house and grounds as a haven for family and visitors rather than running a dump, giving your employer his money's worth, being prompt for appointments, are a few of the many living values needing touted. Most important is giving our children love in time, attention and sensible discipline, in place of hanging them out to dry, as has become the hurtful norm while parents ruin their health and dispostions running in the rat race of discontent.

By remaining quiet, we elders allowed God to be booted out of schools. "Children should get their religious training in church and at home," say the experts and the ACLU blowhards, apparently unaware that many youngsters aren't taken to church and many parents are faithless.

We've not fussed enough about a host of things we should never have tolerated. We're paying for it in worry, fear, loneliness and in a cold, detached, vacuous daze that's rapidly spawning mental and physical violence that soon may be beyond our control.

Of course there are wonderful things that have evolved. I'm not a terminal pessimist by any means. However, I cling to keeping what works--we still use a rotary phone. I vow to go to my grave never having owned a credit card, never having pumped gasoline and never getting laced to a computer. Frankly, I'm upset that my dentist no longer has a spit sink. Those things beat the new suction sweeper things that threaten to dislodge your taste buds. I'd rather fight ropes of saliva sliding into the charming sink. Nor do I like being dumped on my back in the new chairs that double as mock chaise longues. The position defies gravity and makes my head ache. Has to be dangerous.

If only we would sift and simplify. For God's sake, the more things you own, the more burdensome they become. God said that, I didn't. From the looks of things, He needs help getting that across. There's also the little matter of learning what's need and what's want. There's the big matter of worshipping youth to the degree of being afraid to be firm with children and ending up being afraid of them. Being so fearful of aging to the extent of killing yourself amid the numerous supposed methods to stop it, is not only futile consuming of precious time, it's nutty.

Time. Quality time. Often suffers and dies from overstuffed planning. If you don't believe it ask the child getting only quality time. In my experience of staying home to raise the children we wanted (Jim helped), quality time just popped up spontaneously within heaps of ordinary hours together. It seldom materialized by being ordered: "I don't want to play 'Scrabble', I've got homework"; or, "Nope, some other time, John's coming over to play catch."

This song is getting longer than it ought. A church prelude is to softly set a mood for meditation, introspection and prayer in preparation for worship. Given a typewriter, instead of the organ, I tend to wax glib and verbose when worked up about something. Writers are told not to preach. However, there comes the time, like now, when the state of man's inhumanity to man and child compels one to scold or feel negligent.

ANNOUNCEMENTS

Prelude .... pg. vii
Sermon .... pg. 1
    Go Sit on a Tact .... pg. 19
    You Don't Say .... pg. 31
    When You Think About It .... pg. 45
Offertory .... pg. 69
Postlude .... pg. 81
Coda .... pg. 97

Favorite Hymns

#1--James #2- Timothy #3- Matthew #4- Nathan

Anthem
"Heaven Sent"- by Meghan, Katie, Colleen, Becky, Ethan, Paige and Cameron.

Granted, I'm opinionated and adore handing out advice--once a teacher, always a teacher. I just can't help it.

Oscar Wilde capsuled two conflicting gems about giving advice: "He knew the precise psychological moment when to say nothing." (Picture of Dorian Gray-1891) The second, in jest but also logical: "I always pass on good advice. It's the only thing to do with it. It is never of any use to one's self." (from "An Ideal Husband"-1895)

The first I fear I don't inherently know, yet surprisingly, I have times when I keep my mouth shut.

Back to the pitch of common courtesy ruled by common sense, neither of which are as common as they once were. The lack of being polite could very well be the cause of the troubles and shootings in schools. The idea of teens bullying and making fun of others to the point of driving them into anger that breeds tragedy paints a hideous picture of parents too busy, Godless, too stupid to teach respect, that in the long run, would be benefical to the parents in days hence.

Toss in the "me first" and "let it all hang out" baloney with the sex-sogged, drug-soaked, apathetic goings on and it has to be harder work being a good parent today than ever before. Laws that take away a parent's control is like having the asylum run by the inmates.

I'm off the soapbox with this quote by Charles F. Kettering: "We should all be concerned about the future because we all will have to spend the rest of our lives there."

An unnamed source takes a swipe at the likes of me and my grumbling and complaining: "The test of good manners is being able to put up pleasantly with bad ones." Isn't there also a saying about bad things happening when good men say nothing?

SERMON

When both the speaker and the audience are confused, the speech is "profound."

Wear your charm bracelet to church. It will amuse an otherwise restless child. (Leary)

"The best answer to give an atheist is to give him a good dinner and ask if he believes there is a cook." (Louis Nizer)

Listening to organ music is such bliss, but the organist occasionally feels like this!

Drawing. <u>by</u> <u>Lois</u> <u>Dobson</u>

During the first 20 years I was an organist-choir director, people entered the sanctuary and were quiet in their personal preparation for worship. Sometime, during the next 21 years, this reverent deportment broke down perhaps encouraged by the invasion of causal dress and people working double hours with no time to see friends except on Sunday mornings.

As parishioners began loosening up, pre-service time began with whispering. Whispering escalated to soft talk, soft talk soon turned to loud chattering mixed with pew hopping. By this time, the organ prelude was judged as an intrusion.

I tried to shame the gabbers by playing more loudly. They talked more loudly yet. Suddenly softening the volume, so they'd hear themselves shouting, failed as well.

One morning I was so aggravated, I abruptly quit playing the prelude, left the organ bench and sat down in a pew. Nobody took notice except for one kind soul worried and asking, "Are you ill?"

"I'm fine. I'm mad. I'm turning red and about to blow up and splatter all over the walls, "I confided, through clenched teeth. "I practiced my prelude like one possessed, it's beautiful, inspiring and not one ear gives a fig."

"I know, dear. I don't know what's wrong with people these days."

We agreed to hush and set a good example whereupon the minister and the choir appeared. Magically, the buzzing ceased and everyone put on their church faces. I returned to the organ and the hour proceeded without incident, not counting an organ cipher howling non-stop through," Take Time To Be Holy", (its message too late to salvage my humor) and the minister upsetting his water glass. As for any cipher, often they're like the stopped clock that's right twice a day. Now and then it harmonized.

During the after church coffee hour, where talk is desired, I collared the board chairman and the minister.

"Short of the ushers handing out gags, how about appealing to the jawing magpies to bottle it during the prelude?"

"Bear in mind, many come to see friends and visit," returned the preacher.

"That's the only reason to attend church?" I was incredulous. "That's the coffee time's job. Please, let's find an answer. You pay me, I practice devotedly to play music conducive to meditation. Either they hush up or I shan't bother preluding."

Neither my lecture nor the two lines in the next newsletter, pleading for quiet, struck a chord; the rattling continued. My blood pressure rose. It was an insult.

Realizing silence befell when the minister and the choir entered, it struck me as reasonable to reverse the order and play the prelude after they came in. It was the solution.

A warning to the fund raising committee thinking about getting together one of those church birthday-anniversary calendars," Careful, they can bite back."

To illustrate: Those with names in bold type don't receive a single card or telephone call from a single church member on their single, special day. And they paid to have this happen? Okay, to balance the slight, those with unraveled hearts may, in their hurt, forget the Golden Rule and treat like with like; get no cards, send no cards.

Now then, a typical birthday calendar month could carry 40 names. Short of being a millionaire with a secretarial staff, finding, paying for and posting that many cards looms as an insurmountable task and one of horrendous expense. Conservatively, 480 cards sent annually would cost $840 and could seriously reduce the church giving of the average income person.

Nor, as long as telephone books exist, can potential card senders whittle down their mailing list with the excuse of no room in the calendar squares for addresses.

Don't think I'm kidding about the monster waiting to attack within these seemingly innocent publications. I witnessed damage done by one our church sponsored. One lady left the church and two former pew pals became completely former.

Once a month widen the coffee hour with a big cake in honor of all that month's birthdayers. Set out a cake-cost collection jar and hope few weasel out of staying around or contributing.

While in the mood to lambast promotional calendars, there's no lack of those silly, hateful ones commanding your every daily move for a month. Generally, these arrive in newsletters from churches, organizations and schools.

Make a quick donation and hide it. Any old day I have time Monday to count all the socks in the dresser drawers and lay back a penny for each pair. And, do I count all the stray singles minus mates the washer ate? I'll mail in my favorite Bible verse for the Advent booklet a Sunday School class is making but not next Tuesday--company's coming. Can't I send it Saturday or hand it over Sunday after church?

The requests go on, two plus 28, giving 30 reasons to question the sanity of these directives, noble as the motive might be.

The most hilarious was issued by a mental health organization. I saved it after scribbling in sassy replies beneath each order. Under Monday's "Take a Walk", I pointed out there was a thunder storm in progress. Tuesday I was to, "READ A BOOK". Due for cataract surgery, I begged for a postponement of that assignment.

The vapid demands went on relentlessly with no regard to the possibility of inclement weather or family and friends living miles away. Thus, wiped from my list, on designated days, were: "TAKE A CHILD FISHING; KISS YOUR CHILD; HAVE A PICNIC;LOOK FOR THE SUNSHINE;TELL MOM YOU LOVE HER(sadly, mine is deceased) ;RIDE A BIKE (don't own one.)"

"THINK HAPPY THOUGHTS; LISTEN TO MUSIC; and the "SMILE" ones weren't over-taxing. I didn't tumble to, 'DO A FAVOR FOR SOMEONE IN YOUR IMMEDIATE FAMILY", in that I do 274 for them every day as it is and I'm as nuts as they don't want me to be if I swell the number. I was also dubious about, "REACH OUT AND TOUCH SOMEONE", the day I was to give a town historical review for elementary students.

You get the drift of my exasperation not eased by the last entry, "VOLUNTEER TODAY, JOIN THE M.H.A." Had I been crazy enough to obey this set of presumptious demands, I'd have been ripe to avail myself instead of their out-patient services.

When about 10, I peeked at the minister giving the benediction and thought his out-stretched, robed arms looked all the world like angel wings. The only drawback was they were black.

Since then, many church robes, for ministers and choir members, are available in a variety of colors. It was a step in the right direction, especially now that black is favored by Satanists and witches.

Much as we think of an angel having wings of white, wouldn't it be novel for robe makers to design the underpart of robe sleeves in rainbow hues seen only when arms are uplifted and wide spread? How pretty this would be.

On the negative side, those making favorable comments would be admitting they were benediction peekers. Therefore, the robe should first be worn at a baptism.

±   ±   ±

"The church is filled with hypocrites," yelleth the critics.
That's where they belongeth," replieth the forgiving.

Moments before church was to begin, one member of the trio I'd appointed to sing a special number, giggled, saying, "Look! The bulletin says we're singing, 'Swine Low, Sweet Chariot'."

"Okay, you darling three little pigs, enunciate like mad and you can vocally make the needed correction," I cajoled.

I'm having trouble with the endless pitch of putting off loving others until you can fully love yourself. The Commandment begins by saying to, "Love your neighbor", before it gets to, "as you love yourself."

Granted, if you don't love yourself, loving your neighbor in the same amount could give the neighbor short shrift. Hey, loving your neighbor as you'd like to love yourself might make you feel so good you'd accomplish both. Waiting to love others, until you're satisfied with yourself, puts everything on hold. In the meantime, your love reflexes and courage are thrown off kilter.

Phony as it sounds, pretending to love a person who's difficult to love may eventually become factual. It's like not wanting to attend a certain social function when you'd rather stay home and read. You reluctantly honor the invitation and then have a marvelous time.

Loving yourself first is akin to running away to "find yourself". The underlying danger of this search, if one's honest, is not liking the self that's found. The whole run away scene is just a poor excuse for a vacation.

What often sends the person on this inward hunt, I've been told, is being fed up with being someone's child, spouse, parent, friend, employee, to the loss of one's personal identity. What's frequently missed here is that one's best identity may very well be the mixture of one's ties to others. Not that a rest isn't needed now and then.

Come on, unless you're having a nervous breakdown, being preoccupied with finding yourself is a risky, selfish, lonely cop out, related to waiting to love yourself. Both pursuits could gobble up an entire lifetime.

"He who is in love with himself has at least this advantage--he won't encounter many rivals," said G.C Lichtenberg in, "Aphorisms", in 1799.

In the 1940's, teenagers sometimes used, "I love me. Whom do you love? Me?", not from vanity but as a weak apology. Now days, this quote affirms the "me first" mindset without a whiff of an apology.

A pox, too, on the newest campaign to elevate self-love now called, "self-esteem". Hearing cheers for shoddy work and attitude today spells disaster in the future. Isn't it more kind and loving to steer people toward gaining self-respect. Because it's earned, it's real, lasts and encourages the attaining of more.

Where on earth have God's capital letters gone? Before umpteen translations were written for the half-illiterate, the Jesus pronouns appeared in St. James, hymns and church bulletins as "He" or "Him". Since the capitals mysteriously slithered off, Scriptural quotes of our highest authority have been reduced to lower case "he" and "him". When one or more "he" is speaking or being spoken of in our modern Bible versions, it's confusing as to which "he" is saying what.

Enter the feminists, and their bent to bury or outshine anything male, and God Himself ends up as an "it". There's nothing like trying to drag Him and His down to our level.

Wondering if somehow computers weren't able to spit out these respectful capitals, I slipped into the church office one day to ask the minister and secretary. "I'm curious about the Almighty being belittled in print." I explained it fitting for us to attempt to help elevate God once again to His deserved place in print.

They said they hadn't noticed the absence of the caps and indeed the in-house machinery could furnish them. I've no idea if anyone else in the congregation was aware of the change but I was pleased.

My pleasure was short lived. A few months later new hymnals arrived. I was miffed to begin with in that as organist-choir director, I'd not been told they were being ordered. Alas, not one hymn in these new books ended with an "Amen". In my indignation and ability to improvise, I added them anyway and the congregation sang them.

"Not all hymn texts warrant an Amen," informed a church musician friend. "Only the ones with lyrics directly from Scripture," she argued.

"Oh, phooey! A hymn without an Amen is like cake without frosting, like hearing only one shoe drop, like no ritard and dancers being left with one foot in the air when the music stops. An Amen puts a comfortable finish on any hymn although it gets pronouced two different ways. You know, "Ah" or "A" but so be it', I grinned, amused to have wiggled in a slight play on words.

In case you don't know, 'Amen' means, 'So be it'," Mary leaped to explain, my reference having gone past her. "And, that's why it isn't required at the close of every hymn."

I insisted it couldn't hurt to somehow agree with what one had just sung, or, if one wasn't willing to attach "so be it", then don't sing the hymn in the first place. After 30 years of liking Amens, particularily after playing a seven verse hymn, meaning I'd played it eight times (counting introducing it) and was completely hymnotized and weary by the time the Amen came to my rescue.

A well paced hymn without a closing cadence rather drops it all over a cliff.

Rodney Dangerfield and copyrights have problems getting respect. There are horrid hordes of people helping themselves to any copyrighted material a copy machine can handle.

Some of the worst offenders reside in our supposed citadels of honestly: churches; schools; libraries and offices.

The copying person wouldn't dream of invading a home and stealing a silver tea set yet will take another's artistic endeavors without a wallop of self-flagellation. Quite often there's a second theft being committed by unathorized use of the copy machine's ink, paper and electric.

In spite of the explanation, "Reproduction of this publication without permission of the copyright owner is a criminal offense subject to prosecution", there are those believing that having bought the book, music or photograph, it's their's to do with what they wish. Externally it is, internally it isn't, if it bears a copyright notice.

Except for the time involved, getting permission to copy isn't all that difficult. A publisher may allow copying in return for a credit line, and/or, a small royalty fee, depending on what's to be done with the material.

How many wonderful future works we may have lost because the talented were so copy-stolen they were forced into other work to earn a living. Copy pilfering robs the creator, the publisher, artists, type setters, press operators, paper companies, etc.-- everyone connected to getting a published piece on the market.

Short of authors, composers, whomever, acting as their own copyright police (it has happened with infringers being sued for large amounts of money), sensible reproaches wither as fast as the copy machine ruffles out copies. Choir director copiers claim they lift anthems because of limited music budgets. Actually, if copying costs were tallied, the copies might not be such a bargain.

A few years ago, some publishers got together and, for a fee paid in advance, allow customers to make additional copies of the scant amount of originals purchased. Sort of the," if you can't beat 'em, join 'em", defense tactic fraught with the fragile notion that it's better to earn a little than nothing whatsoever.

There's an amazing, or feigned, amount of ignorance about the meaning of "copyright". Maybe it's a borderline oxymoron suggesting that the notice should read," copywrong."

Me thinks scolding about this is futile. I'm sure it is, judging how many times I've caught copiers in the act only to field gales of laughter after imparting my boring lecture. Running in a new angle of," one day there'll be nothing to copy because the inventive guys will hang it all up if what they churn out they know is going to be pilfered", doesn't penetrate an inch.

It's a waste of breath for present day social reformers to object to the "birds of a feather flock together" reality. A roomful of strangers soon cluster into small groups, drawn together by tone of voice, vocabulary, dress, body build and perhaps by the unconscious sniff--you know, the chemical attraction scientists investigate along with cow farts.

Anyway, with discrimination of any kind now a "no-no", we once had a minister determined to have no cliques within the church family. He was pumped up to melt the congregation into one homogenous bunch by God and for God. It didn't gel.

Few wanted to have a joint New Year's Eve party to the exclusion of family and pals of another religious persuasion. The 65 year old Sunday School class members didn't cotton to including 20 year olds of all mouth and no experience into their discussions. The 20's group felt the same, in reverse.

What the pastor failed to see were the wonderful strengths coming from the wonderful differences. He didn't reckon with the power of kindred souls liking and needing to be kindred: a committee of like minds, gets a lot done in a hurry and

8

with less wrangling.

He finally gave up and everyone gravitated back to their assorted flock slots with glee and rejoicing.

The government keeps trying to stir us into one indistinguishable broth, too, in spite of the lure of genes, tastes or whatever keeps us interestingly diverse.

We need some sort of campaign to slow down our national rush to forgive any and everyone of any and every rotten thing they do. It's become epidemic.

It's appalling to hear a parent offering blanket forgiveness to some madman who's killed her child two days ago. First of all, when the murderer hasn't asked for absolution, handing it out quickly is unfair to the child's memory.

How can shock and unfathomable agony spawn genuine forgiveness in a matter of hours? Doesn't doing so send the wrong message to criminals?

Forgiving, to be real, takes time, as does grieving, as does reform on the part of the forgiven. Vindicating too quickly borders on aiding, abetting and condoning.

I'm not against forgiving, so don't write me a letter. It's just that it's not easy and hurrying it could be to one's peril. Society's absorbtion with coddling bad kids, rude adults and ingrates, no matter what evil they've perpetrated, smells of self-congratulatory grandiosity.

Racing to forgive even one's self for minor behavorial errors isn't a good idea: no guilt, no learning.

Let's assume the news in Christmas card letters is factual in detailing successes of family members, pets and belongings. Let's imagine that those receiving such letters detest and debunk each as pure braggadocio, lacking substance. Translation: a pack of lies.

This being substantiated, let us offer to enroll the disgruntled readers in the study course, "How to Handle Success--Other People's."

The first lesson explains how there's no merriment, December 25, Jan. 1, Easter or May 20,for those denied sharing each jot, tittle, corpuscle and globule of all positive conquests so vast they've earned the right to flow forth from pen to paper. Each recorded layer serves to obliterate all specks and flecks of any foozied fiasco, big, small, remembered, forgotten or imagined.

Lesson II concentrates on the necessity for anyone, battered by boasts, to boost their concentrational powers of pretending up to new and amicable heights. In layman's terms, make believe you're as happy for the orator as he, she or they are for heself, sheself or themself, including the dogself, catself, carself and new stuff stuff's self.

The wondrous teaching within this lesson is: what starts out to be a self-deluding sham, when practiced long enough, converts to genuine pleasure for both letter writer and pretender, the latter now devoid of pretense and tense tenseness. In lessor laymen's terms, jealously is overcome when you come over to exchanging green eyes for true blue, as in blue blood of good breeding, which anyone with red blood should therefore desire.

Lesson IV is instrumental in learning to understand why it's understandable and not inharmonious for one to blow or toot one's own horn.

Faced with others turning deaf ears, blind eyes, walking past, instead of jumping on another's hard-built bandstand, there's no recourse for the unattended, unnoticed, but to make a grand stand and trumpet his, her, their, triumphs in the vain hope of being heard and securing a place in life's orchestra of recognition and inspiration.

The teacher suggests this behavior is like going for an audition without an appointment. In laymen laymen's language, like the horn owner seeking emergency attention when sad, angry and feeling ignored.

Lesson V summarizes the values of being joyous over another's accomplishments and acquisitions, knowing full well none grew on trees. We're to memorize the fact that the tree had to be planted, fertilized, watered, pruned, picked, and sheltered. That's enough energy expended to make anyone tired of not hearing applause. Surely once, at Christmastime, Jan. 1, Easter and May 20, even Sept.19, ego puff-piece author-horn sounders are to be forgiven and smiled upon. One might go so far as to offer congratulations. (Sept. 19, is just any old day, like all others, not to be envious.)

Lesson VI is adamant: anyone composing a similar news

letter, is instructed not to dispatch it to anyone in crisis. In plain language, refrain from sending the cussed, fool thing to anyone down on his luck.

Underscore, in your self-help text book, the section ending with," The success of someone I know sets an example." It's saying: "If they can do it, so can I." Perchance you wouldn't enjoy a carload of anything resembling their gains, salute the flag of, "To each his own," and just be glad you re thought of enough to be in their address book.

You're only recourse, if you fail the class, is to read their Christmas letter, grind your teeth and tear it up. Unless you intend to one-up them by writing them a note of your own. Then, it's helpful to have their letter in front of you to pinpoint, one by one, things you plan to top.

It's very difficult to "love your neighbor as yourself" when your neighbor isn't one speck as nice as you are. Further compounding the issue is the fact that this particular neighbor doesn't like you one little bit.

Both true and blue: you're never completely your own person until after your parents die. If both parents have had a normal life span and you're anticipating the same, you've only about 15 years before you feel your middle aged children have figured this out for themselves.

What they haven't anticipated yet is how much they'll miss you in a zillion ways. It's a strange independence with unexpected holes in it. More strange, and containing bigger holes, is the day when no one's alive who knew your parents.

This is the most final, lonely disconnect imaginable. Gone is the opportunity to share memories of them with others cognizant of personalities. Gone is the chance to add to your memories of your parents by virtue of relatives and friends who knew them well.

When you find yourself in these circumstances, you'll honor them by intutively emulating their values. By becoming more and more like them, you keep them alive as you, someday, will be by your children.

When asked what you charge to give a program, a talk, whatever, for a church or organization, it's wise to ask, "What do you usually pay?"

Tell them what you charge, which you're prone to set depending on what the group personally means to you and so it varies, and you could miss getting much more without strain on their part.

If what they usually pay is too low to interest you, say so, quote something higher and be ready to be fired before you're hired.

Program seekers believing "God-given" talents should always be donated aren't being just or fair. Most talents have taken years and money to hone into being thought of as Godgiven, no matter how much proclivity was put in by God.

Talented hobbists are natural targets for being expected to appear without remuneration. "It'll be good advertising," the program director enthuses, knowing full well it will take two days to pack up one's display wares, a tank of gasoline to get there, lunch to buy, and a baby sitter to pay upon return home.

Church fathers aren't immune to hoping the organist-choir director will appear twice every week for the next 20 years without a salary. "It can be considered as your church giving," the, over thrifty zealots might run past the applicant.

If the organist-choir person succumbs, it means the church never gets that giving increased. Dismissed in this approach is that the musician might be a tither and the higher the pay, the more the church's ten percent becomes. Many tithers have determined that the tithe is just paying what one owes, giving is above and beyond the ten percent.

Lastly, it's not smart to have unpaid staff. They're not as motivated to show up and do what's expected, as is the person being paid. And, how do you fire a volunteer? It's not realistic in regard to budget expectations in the future, either.

A few church officials don't like hiring their own church members for the same firing troubles that might arise. We professional musicians don't enjoy the free fingered ones thinking we're heathens because we charge.

It would be dishonorable for me to address anything musical without crediting my unforgettable piano-organ teacher and my mother, Laura.

Mother was an accomplished, trained singer and a good pianist. Dad played a banjo , the piano and a saxaphone, fast and loud. At age four, I was taken across the street for piano lessons with Katherine (Kit) McVey, who'd returned here after losing her hearing that ended her concert career.

I was nearsighted but no one knew it, nor did I. You never miss an elephant unless you've had one and I didn't know what I should be seeing. I dutifully gazed at the pages on the music rack and didn't see a thing. I did rather wonder why I was told to fasten my eyes there instead of watching my hands. Anyway, not seeing developed my ear; Kit and mother played my little pieces and I copied the sound. My problem was discovered when I was in third grade and my desk seat moved farther back from the blackboard.

Getting glasses was a marvel. Trees tops had leaves, birds flew high and music pages were alive with little black golf clubs. Learning to read notes was as thrilling as seeing the world in focus.

Working with Kit, 14 years as one of her 40 weekly piano students and six years as her organ pupil, was an exceptional adventure. A tall, large bosomed, loud speaking woman, Kit made lessons exciting by choosing a wide variety of music and adding interesting tales about composers. To supplement her income, Kit, a good cook, built a catering business. "If you hold your mouth right, I'll give a taste," she'd promise students after lessons.

Kit taught by placing one hand on the edge of the piano. She could feel the vibrations and would catch mistakes no matter how hard I tried to skim through a tough section by playing it extremely fast. When she went to the kitchen to stir soup, I'd leave Bach in the lurch and thump out Boogie Woogie. "Norma, get back to Bach this instant," she'd holler, having felt the tempo change through her feet.

Kit had studied lip reading and "saw" everything anyone said. This was a worry for people at a party and half a room away from Kit. One didn't dare say a word they didn't want her to see.

When Kit sang with a student's lesson song and was off key, it meant the piano needed tuned. She had absolute pitch. She played the local church organ until a week before she died, taught herself to cane chairs and played the organ for silent movies in a nearby city. She occasionally consented to play a concert and would have me go along with the driver and her so I could check the piano's good and bad points. For organ recitals I was appointed to report if a pipe ciphered or a rank was out of tune. She and mother managed to give me the work-life I cherish to this day.

Purlioned from a church bulletin: I can tell you what's wrong with the country. Most everybody wants a job that pays more than the average person is worth, and it's got to be a job that has someone else around to do the work, and that someone has got to take the blame when things get messed up because the first somebody didn't do what he was hired to get done." (no name given)

I played my first wedding at age 13. It went well until the groom, best man and minister failed to recognize, "To a Wild Rose"-- a number they said they knew and their cue to take their places prior to the wedding march.

Before starting, "Rose", for the third time, I tried turning my head to see where these people might be but couldn't see around the brim of my large picture hat. Mother had attended rehearsel so was aware of the plan. Realizing the problem, she left her seat and prodded the late comers down the aisle.

I was given a string of pearls for supplying the music. Some 20 strings later, I began charging a fee. The fee has increased over the years but hardly adequate when a non-musical vocalist has to be taught the bride-chosen selections note by note and fifty times through.

One doesn't play many weddings before meeting a bride who's dismayed upon learning that her organist expects to be paid. This is puzzling and a bit insulting when a bride fully anticipates paying the florist, cake maker, tuxedo shop, reception hall owner, caterer, minister, photographer, bridal shop, hair dresser, church janitor and whomever else's "work" is needed. Really, wedding musicians do double duty if slated to attend the rehearsel and triple if practice is needed to handle an unfamiliar organ, especially the wee ones with not enough keyboard to traverse the "Lord's Prayer's" high notes. Re-arranging the music ahead of time is preferable to suddenly trading notes for a handful of air.

Organs with popsicle stick foot pedals, the slippery ones that send a foot slithering, present a challenge to anyone unaccustomed to this design. Pianists confronted with out of tune, key sticking, broken damper pedal pianos with cracked sounding boards shouldn't be begrudged their pay either. Real mental anguish results from doing battle with a faulty instrument along with the vain hope that the music isn't as frightful to hear as to produce. In such a situation, it's understandable to pray that most of the guests remember having previously heard you playing a top-notch instrument on a fine finger day!

Most church musicians are privy to strange happenings that have occured during church services, funerals and weddings. Unless truly tragic, most mistakes are harmless errors born of being human. Often, they're silently greeted and enjoyed by guests as sort of ice breaker, stress relief episodes. To all but those in charge of the ceremony, and/or to the goofing goofer, all devoid of a sense of humor.

Four weddings in one day were managed by the times chosen for each. The first at 10:30 a.m, noon for the second, the third set for 3:30 p.m., the last at 7:30 p.m. Thankfully, all were within a seven mile radius of our home, enabling me to slip in between the last two in order to catch my breath, put my feet up and eat.

One bride, wishing to have, "Hard Headed Woman", and, "Fool On the Hill", sung, prompted me to suggest she get the minister's approval. She didn't. The moral of the story is to speak up when you believe certain choices have no rightful place in a religious setting and would curl your hair no matter where you were subjected to it.

It's nearly impossible to explain to lovers of today's music how playing the sheet music version doesn't compare with how the tune sounded when performed by the group that popularized it. Minus the drums, guitars and breath catching wailings, the things are left with only sparse, unresolved chords, or merely intervals, above a bass line that defies all logic pertaining to counting. The beats, in such opposition to those of the natural world, reduce me to a complaining pulp. I just flat out refuse to play some of them and wish more churches would follow the lead of those who've compiled lists of acceptable wedding music and that's that.

During an outdoor wedding, wind blew my music into a neighboring field. I improvised while a guest galloped through the weeds to catch and return it. Heavy duty tape or spring clothes pins can anchor wind threatened pages. Just don't stick up pages that will need turned!

A groom hadn't been informed that the bride's mother had hired a clown to hand out balloons for guests to loose at the close of the ceremony. Outraged, he raged, "What is this? A damned kid's birthday party?" He was so furious, he refused to pose for photographs that included his new mother-in-law. Also, his bride wanted a photo of herself with her horse and he wasn't thrilled about that either.

As the tenor aimed for a high note, his bow tie came unhooked, sailed from his collar, over the choir loft rail to land on the floor at the feet of the best man.

When the couple knelt for a prayer, the groom's shoe soles were seen to bear bold magic marker words of, "Help", on one, "Me", on the other. Giggles erupted causing the preacher, not in on the joke, to immediately, and obviously, check his fly.

A four year old flower girl, standing quietly with the other attendants, suddenly announced, in forte, "I gotta pee." An adult female guest deftly led the child to a rest room. Everyone pretended they hadn't heard. Nice.

Helping our son, Nate, as his backup wedding photographer, I hustled to a nearby store to buy more film after we learned that all sets of parents and grandparents were divorced from one another and had no intention of posing together for any family group shots. This resulted in taking the bride and groom and her mother, the bride and groom and her father, etc., etc., etc. This ate up film and time and so flustered the couple as to nearly wreck their day. Wouldn't you have thought they could have been congenial for one moment??

"Who giveth this woman to be married to this man?", inquired the minister. "Her mother, her father and I," returned the father, to the horror of his faithful wife.

After kissing his daughter, Dad, while backing toward his seat, stepped on her veil, which pulled off her headpiece He replaced it and then repeated the entire mishap again.

Bless the bride who says, "It's up to you. Whatever you play will be fine with me."

"Great!", is my quick and sincere reply, whereupon I assure her it will be a mix with something for everyone.

"Something for everyone," was Kit's advice. "The smart bride picks a song or two that will please her Grandma. It's a small concession to make to be kept in her will." The flippant reference to Grandma's will was said in jest.

However, one needn't be a genius to know that presenting a wide and varied menu of music for a gathering of hearts and ears of various ages and tastes has its benefits: when the second song deviates in tempo, registration and dynamics of distinctly different, but suitable, flavor from the first one, attention is apt to improve. Granted, a few may be cloaking their disgust in quietness--the best mode in which to be critical--but that's all right because the next song should repair the damage; the real reason to run through a gamut of classical to something contemporary, is the hope that one or two hearts will be moved by one or two offerings they plug into because they recognize the melodies or, if not, find them appealing anyway.

Lastly, and not to be discounted, unless we're freakishly modest, are the compliments gleaned from giving an all encompassing program. We're dead if we don't draw inspiration and pleasure from accolades as simple as. "I liked the music." We're lazy if we hug appreciatve remarks to our bosoms and forget to keep practicing and expanding our music libraries.

Wedding related typographical errors are an enigma unto themselves. "Altar" frequently gets altered to "alter" and a bride and attendants floating down the "isle" is sometimes recorded. A newlywed was not amused to read the newspaper write-up that told readers her gown was trimmed in "lice". How about, "The pre-nuptial solos were 'dung' by the bride's cousin"?

During my 20 year stint of news writing, too often my typewriter wrote "group sinning" for " group singing" and more than a few couples were married in the

"Untied" Presbyterian or Methodist church. Blessed with an ardent editor, these seldom got into print however often they popped up in my original copy. Needless to say, having made many has made me more tolerant of printed errors.

Marrying a printer has reaped me a fifty one year bonus of having an expert, in-house proof reader. Jim's also an excellent speller. I'm not, so what good is a dictionary when a word's beginning letters are as elusive as the remaining ones? Jim to the rescue when I have sense enough to consult him. Poor Jim spent years reciting the individual letters of "Baccalaureate", to protect my news writing reputation, only to have the government banish the school rite before I could spell it on my own.

I shrink from discussing wedding reception music only to admit being highly agitated by the volume of most I've had the misfortune to endure. On a wedding gig with Nate, we found it refreshing when a bride's father, with her permission, paid and then promptly, dismissed the band, all of whom ignored his request to, "Tone it down so people can talk."

It's a shame for relatives to arrive from all corners of the world and be unable to exchange a discernible word.

Skipping back to brides and their desires for music the organists, pianists or soloists don't have and never want to own. Make it clear that it's up to the bride to supply these. Once upon a time, the bride's parents paid for everything, including attendants' gowns. No self-respecting groom would ask his best man and ushers to pay tuxedo rental charges. It was deemed an imposition to "honor" friends by "inviting" them to be part of your gala and then rudely stick it to 'em financially.

In fact, I can remember when a fellow didn't wear a tuxedo to any big "do" unless it was his own tux. A good suit and a shoe shine sufficed for the middle income men. It's a wonder the affluent haven't all taken to donning suits in retaliation for being copied under false pretenses.

Honestly, this formal garb has been so overworked as to ring with overtones of Hallowe'en. The day four, big men, each stuffed into a lime green tux below a pink, ruffled shirt, strolled forward to join the groom, their appearance was nothing short of high comedy, spotlighted by the bilious color combination of their "costumes".

Before working numerous weddings as Nate's assistant, I had no idea how many organists play the instrument as they would a piano. The piano's damper pedal sustains tones to create a legato, smoothly flowing line of music. This is done on an organ by creeping, crawling and exchanging fingers to get where you're going without letting go of anything more than melody notes on the way. Lifting the hands up and down, as done playing the piano, turns what ought to be legato into bumps with staccato silences in between. For those who've not studied organ, try playing the example below. The finger exchanges appear in parenthesis.

You'll soon get the hang of it and find it easier than anticipated. Remember, your hands act as the damper pedal an organ doesn't have. Thus, glide, don't strike the keys except when dynamic markings so indicate.

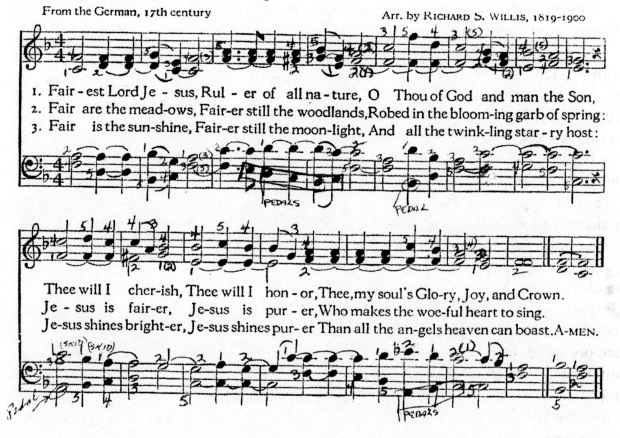

These fingerings are only sugggestions but convey the idea of how to wiggle around exchanging a finger down with another taking its place while the note is still sounding. Now the replaced finger or fingers are free to tip into the upcoming notes without having to lift the hand and create a break of tone.

Depending on your hand and finger span, practice creeping with finger exchanges that are not terribly uncomfortable. It does seem awkward at first but you'll get used to doing it and like the glassy, smooth tone flow this creates. You may still lift hands at the end of musical phrases, where singers would naturally take a breath, to reposition fingers.

Bass notes written lower than a hand can reach within a chord or interval, should either be played on the foot pedals or raised an octave within range of what would be the tenor line.

Notice all notes being immediately repeated are tied with the exception of the melody notes. You may, if the tempo indicates, strike anew some of the repeated chords to keep singers from dragging.

17

GO SIT ON A TACT

Social tact is making your company feel at home, even though you wish they were." (Anonymous)

"Silence is not always tact; and it is tact that is golden, not silence," (Samuel Butler)

Tact is the ability to describe others as they see themselves." (Abraham Lincoln)

Lori is having troubles of some sort. You bake her a wondorous cake, from scratch. You deliver it. You know your good deed gift is appreciated.

Two hours later Lori phones. Amid giggles, she tells, "The funniest thing happened! On my way to the table with your gorgeous cake, I tripped over the dog and the cake landed upside down in the middle of the floor. Isn't that a riot? The cake was wrecked and the carpet's a mess."

It's hardly fun or funny learning your work, time, expense and good intentions aborted and created a cleaning chore for your weary friend in the bargain.

Please, let givers be spared hearing of any disaster that befalls a gift. Better Lori had said, " Thanks so much for the cake. It was a work of art and someday I'd like to have the recipe."

If there's anything I hate, it's a two-edged compliment cut through with surprise and amazement.

Examples: "My dear, don't tell me you prepared this delicious lunch all by yourself?"; "The house tour was truly great. I had no idea there were such nice homes in this small town of yours."; "Now tell me the truth. Did you honestly make that outfit or do you have a seamstress you haven't told me about?"

First, it's disheartening not to be believed. Secondly, being so merrily clobbered makes it clear that you've been thought of as less than capable.

Consider the source and say nothing. Or, if this undeserved, piled on, overboard astonishment prickles your humble pride, even out the flaying field and reply. Something like, " Your dismay is downright insulting.", lends a certain balance.

It's a shame when people are moved to say something nice and don't stop while they're ahead. For instance, Anne arrived at the party sporting a new, short haircut. Ruthie enthused, "Oh, Anne, I love your new cut."

"Thank you," smiled Anne.

Whereupon, hairbrained Ruthie blundered on, "I really hated it when it was long." (boo)

Julie to the rescue. " I thought your long do was very attractive." Quick to realize this could mean she didn't like Anne's short hair, Julie added, "I also think this style is elegant." The, "also", covered all bases. Saved by the belle with hair trigger sense.

And then there are the souls bent on adding confessions to compliments. Jane gushes to Sue," I'm so glad I've had the chance to get to know you, Sue. You're quite down to earth and not at all as stuck up as I'd expected you'd be."

How can Sue erase the snob slap? "I hope you aren't in the habit of making accusations without evidence," is a hint Jane would do well taking to heart.

Much as Sue yearns to say, "Well, I guess you're not a good judge of character," this might pop Sue right back into her old expectations of Sue being top lofty.

Nobody wins when well intended remarks prattle around an unnecessary corner. How about the nominating committee chairman phoning and running her mouth to defeat?

"Hello, Dorothy, the 'Do Righters' would like you to be the new secretary. I do hope you'll accept the nomination."

Dorothy is pleased until the numbskull nominator adds, "You're the seventh person we've asked."

Until this untidy clue was dropped, Dorothy was thinking she might enjoy the secretarial position. Now her brain goes into overdrive and she ponders: playing second fiddle is one thing but seventh? Claiming other obligations, she declines wishing she had the nerve to tell Miss Nominator to take her seventh place steno pad and stick it up her orchestra pit.

Ministers can be equally as graceless. You'd think a seminary would have a course in place to support, "the less said, the better."

Instead of simply thanking the substitute organist for playing, Rev. Biglippy seemed hell bent to explain it to death.

"When I heard Mary couldn't be with us today, I called nine other organists. None were free to help us out today in Mary's absence. As a last resort (this is the rude word quartet), I got ahold of George and he consented to help us out. Thank you George, we're glad to have you with us."

What a glorious welcome Everyone knew George was one of the best organists in the area. "As a last resort..."? He should have been asked first. So should have the prospective "Do Righter secretary with super credentials as a past secretary to a company CEO.

No, The Rev. Mr. Biglippy wasn't a member of the "Do Righters". His error, too, was spewing unnecessary details. It's to George's credit that he played the hymns at a singable pace. He must have been tempted to crank up the tempo and leave Biglippy breathless and faint trying to keep up with, "Be Not Dismayed Whate'er Betide".

It's horrible being with four friends all of whom discuss in minute detail what they did together last week before jumping ahead to discuss what fun they're going to pursue next week. The rub is, you weren't included last week and no invitation is extended for the upcoming one.

If you've never had this happen, either you're deaf or blessed with flawless friends worthy of your undying devotion and respect.

Another common 'friendly'?) gaffe sometimes heard in introductions: Friend #1 and #2 run into Friend #3, a good, good friend of #1 who's never met # 2. With cheer and gusto, friend #1 says, "Friend #3, I want you to meet my very best in the world, Friend #2".

It's 1,2,3, and Friend #3 is out, as the good, good, maybe best, in her mind, friend of #1, losing her status to #2. To thicken the plot, #2 feels guilty for usurping #3 and is now obligated to do her best to be best, moreso than before this mantle of superiority was cast over her shoulders by #1.

Oh, the unrelenting pressure we heap on others merely because we over speak. Adjectives need omitted or used sparingly lest they stir up unwanted competition.

I learned, doing news reporting, never to write, "This year's town Christmas decorations are the prettiest ever seen," or, "Tommy Johns has the best baseball stats ever recorded at the high school." Positive statements of this caliber beg for someone to pounce forward to prove otherwise.

A liberal use of "qualifers" (possibly; one of; maybe; perhaps; probably;) furnish escape hatches for writers and speakers. Adopt and use them generously.

It's also wise (not 'probably' wise, one hundred percent wise) never to preface a story by announcing it's funny. Again, you're asking for disagreement by being so darned confident. No one relishes being told how they should react before knowing what the dickens the act is.

The club secretary reads, "Everyone enjoyed the annual picnic", and up jumps Eddie to tell all, "Any old day I enjoyed the picnic, I got stuck with most of the work."

Eddie's honesty was acceptable because he didn't name names and didn't say he got stuck with "all" the work.

Isn't is a bother not being able to come with a snappy comeback? Probably, (off the hook again with that qualifier, I hope), the majority of us think of the perfect punch line three hours or three days after we've stopped sulking, seething, brooding, hurting enough to regain our wits and wit.

I speak rapidly and get ribbed about it constantly. My retort, when criticized? "No, I don't talk fast, you listen slowly."

I'm an avid miniaturist, with a shop no less. Bunches of adults and youngsters are equally as addicted as I. Others, who think we're nutty, love accusing us of being in our second childhoods. After regaling them with seventeen reasons miniatures also fascinate many historians, artisans, hobbists and children, Leonardo daVinci's quote is the topper: "Small things concentrate the mind." I love it!

Admittedly I'm, "following my bliss", as advocated by the late Joseph Campbell, teacher and philosopher. He thought everybody, at one time or another, should follow their bliss as long as it wasn't against their moral values or financial security.

Uncanny how many non—celebrity people have unlisted telephone numbers. For all the nuisance calls they escape, they have to be missing invitations and newsy things they'd enjoy.

When my secretive friends need reached, I'm often phoned. "Do you have John's number? I really need to get in touch with him to ask if he'll speak at our seminar."

"Yes, I have it but I'm not allowed to give it to anyone. Give me your number and I'll have him call you."

I get John's answering machine. Five hours later, the seminar woman rings me again. I vow I've tried finding John and promise to try again. Two more tries. I finally get him on the third, having hung up during the previous two before the recorded message kicked in.

Ready to recite the number John needs, I can't find it. Matt or Jim must have mixed it up in their papers or thrown it away. I ask, they don't know. It's not in the waste basket. Not sandwiched in the clutter on the desk. Next, I run the sweeper to redd up (we, in Pennsylvania 'redd' up things, we also 'worsh' our clothes and go wading in the crick') the snippets that tumbled out of the waste basket.

Fifteen minutes later, the lady's number is found marking a page in the book I've been reading. I do my duty and call John again. I get his answering machine but he's kidding, he's home and comes on.

Three weeks later this scenario begins again. The chairperson needs to run last minute details past John. Now John has misplaced the woman's number and can't remember her last name. I suggest he phone the church, where the event's to be held, and inquire. He does, and calls me back to say he got their answering machine and left my number.

The church secretary finally reaches me and after being held up twice by rude "calls waiting", I get the information. I relay it to John's answering machine. Gloriously, this brought an end to my serving beyond the call of duty until two days later:" Norma, since you're a friend of Jane Hidenseek, do you have her unlisted number?"

I quoted it, imploring the person not to tell how she got it.

Please, please, don't call Linda and ask, "What are you wearing to Sue's party Saturday night?"

Linda hasn't been invited and there you are with your mouth now big enough to swallow all of Asia. You've also managed to paint Sue black.

I was personally put on the spot when Evelyn asked me, "Why aren't Bill and Marie here tonight?"

Other guests grew quiet as I, not anxious to admit Bill and Marie hasn't been invited, groped for an answer.

"Bill and Marie had other plans," was my lame reply, not wanting Evelyn to know Bill and Marie had been to a shindig of ours the week before to which Evelyn and Jake hadn't been invited. Bill can't stand Jake.

Later, I told Evelyn, "You know, short of renting a hall, there's no way a host can invite everyone to each and every gathering." I hoped she got the drift and won't question anyone else's guest list.

Store owners beware: store building entrance doors so heavy a lone woman can't open them without throwing full body weight at 40 miles an hour against them is bad for business.

Having good china and not using it more often is short changing family and friends. Frangible dishes demand careful handling. In turn,this demands attention to what's being served and the fancy aura of the meal, or tea time, is the more savored.

Melodic door chimes and tuneful car horns play too many tune fragments.Short is okay but the inventors should arrange the bits to resolve rather than quit on leading tones.

If I were a nudist, I'd invent a pubic hair toupee for older members surprised to find baldness can also occur in that particular, personal area.

Modern home designers might pencil in dumb waiters and laundry shoots as "new" features in house plans. Reinstating these would save the housewife many trips up and down stairs. Both could be outfitted with toddler proof screens. Then a conveyor belt to carry washed, folded clothes to the second floor would be helpful, too.

Because our kitchen sink drain baskets mysteriously wind up out of their assigned cavities, I'm after a plumber who will agree to weld them to their seats. Or, should plumbers be accused of liking straying baskets that assure future service calls?

Why wash your hair and body everyday if neither is dirty? Ask most dermatologists and hear how you're flushing away valuable body oils without which one day you'll dry up and blow away. Washing a clean body doesn't give one a sense of accomplishment so why waste the time, soap and water unless you're bored or cold?

Laugh all you want about saving and reusing gift wrapping paper and ribbons, ironing them, if necessary, but it saves trees and enough money to spend more on the. It's thrift in motion. I get razzed unmercifully about it.

I'm also content wearing 35 year old clothes that looked good then and still do. Being prudent isn't being stingy. Someone who's stingy cuts the buttons off the coat she's giving to the poor.

Let's resolve to argue with people who have a skewed hate for the rich. They rant about a lavish party that cost thousands of dollars and howl that the money should have been given to those in abject poverty. Tell that to the caterer, florist, musicians, grocer, and all having a bill to present to the party throwers.

Leaning upon the theory of financial sages, explain that if all the world's money was divided equally among us it would be a pitifully small stipend apiece. Nor would it be long before the most capable and brightest, those having the most to begin with, would find ways to get it back.

There are hate-the-rich gripers who revel in a wealthy person's tragedy with a cock-eyed, mean declaration: "Aha, see, money can't buy health or happiness," quoted in a tone that hints it's wiser and less troublesome not to be well heeled. Sort of congratulating one's noble self for not having or wanting money, forgetting, conveniently, that human hurts happen to all no matter what their social status. Real compassion is due everyone and I don't know a single rich person who escapes the kinds of troubles that befall all of us.

As for Scripture warning about riches, there's also the parable of the talents (money) that needs reviewed. Many of the affluent have the talent to earn and the talent to invest their talents (money) with gobs to give away. The more they give away the more they're blessed to earn, invest and give again. This shouldn't irk anyone.

For the handful of pea brains bragging about not being rich, don't you wonder if they had their druthers if they'd rather be sick and poor or sick and rich?

My kingdom for a sweeper cord long enough to praddle clear across two rooms and attachements that would stay on without bindings of duct tape, doors with knobs high enough not to jump into my pockets, an electric can opener with cord long enough to skid the whole works to the edge of a counter so a tall can may be hung over the edge (into mid air) in order to have room for the can lid to get under the cutting part.

Have you tried to buy a refrigerator without a freezer compartment, especially when you have a big freezer elsewhere in your house and don't need another"?

Are you fed up with buying "new and improved" only to deduct it's been made "old and bad" and costs more?

When you eat in a self-serve place, do you resent leaving a tip when it's really you who has earned it?

Imagine the blow to a homely person's ego when cast to play the role of the ugly person. I keep hoping the actor's awful on-screen or stage face is due to the work of a talented make-up artist. If not, the actor has found the courage to turn a disadvantage into a plus.

What are we going to do with historians tinkering with the lives and reputations of statesmen I'd been taught were of upstanding character? It's hateful to think George never cut down the cherry tree and so had nothing to not lie about.

What a disappointment to entertain written thoughts that some founding fathers were fathers fond of fondling the founding ladies. Worse is the report about the Erie man finding hundreds of errors in school text books.

"Never spank or hit a child," says the childless child pyschologist, "it only proves that you're bigger and stronger".

That's true and I'm glad to be bigger or I'd be in danger.

A toddler can't fathom what a car will do to him if he trundles into the middle of a busy road. Being killed or smushed he doesn't comprehend. However, a swift swat he understands and soon reasons that being in the street is asking for another and is reason enough not to go there.

The great "how to hang the toilet paper" harangue has wiped itself out and we should rejoice that Congress somehow managed to stay out of the issue of the tissue. As of now, you can hang it any danged way you like.

Let's not be duped by dog owners walking the dog to exercise it. We suspect it's to have the dog deposit its "do" in someone else's yard.

Strange that men have "jobs", women have careers

I hate the power struggle game of a hostess trying to get a dieter to eat something he or she shouldn't--a diabetic, for instance. "Surely you can eat this just this once," she minces, " I made it and do want you to at least taste it." In the mean meantime, the guest is reminded of his illness and has to mention it to get out of obeying the order.

Grown children aren't thrilled to have you begin, "Now, when I was a kid," unless they're specifically asking for a childhood story of yours. Do this often and they'll wish you'd never been a kid. I think it's because they interpret what we tell as being critical of their times and happenings in comparison. It gets their backs up when you spout how many miles you walked to school in four feet high snow. They feel we think their slackers by riding the bus-- a bus they've no choice but to take since it was their elders who thought up the bus travel in the first place.

You're smart to keep lists of the daily news bites you've told your adult babies so you don't repeat yourself and watch their eyes glaze over.

The agony of being stood up needs to be told to my stander upper. The audacity of someone inviting themselves to stop in at three o'clock and never show up, never phone to say they're not coming by.

I run the sweeper, bake brownies polish the tea pot, comb my hair and postpone two un-urgent errands only to to wait and wait and reluctant to start anything else lest they do turn up.

Two days later, the date and time setter sees me at the post office and says, " I hope it didn't matter that I didn't get there the other day. I decided to go shopping with Roberta."

Girded by the bravery of age and the power of truth, I return, "Yes, it did. I cancelled errands, swept, baked, combed and waited." I intended to appear as exasperated as I felt, now multiplied by learning I'd been cast aside for Roberta, nice as she is. Really, we shouldn't pretend it was agreeable. It wasn't and we shouldn't promote more such laxness by being over gracious about any act of rudeness.

The teacher asked his high schoolers asked how they might handle a hypothetical emergecy; "What would you do if you were lost in the woods?"

A young man volunteered, "I'd get a mirror and flash an 'S.O.L.' sign."

The same teacher, my brother-in-law, assigned essays and received one entitled, "My S.A."

I can't make fun remembering asking my husband, "Who on earth is "Detente"?

Five year old Tommy promised his mother he'd sit still and be quiet during the funeral--the first he'd attended.

Elsie, the organist, was 80 years old, very thin and wrinkled. She'd recently sustained a neck injury and her neck was splinted by a complicated metal cage affixed to her head and shoulders.

Tommy was quiet until he spied Elsie. In a loud voice, he inquired, "Mommy, why is that dead lady wired to the organ?"

Until television cameras began scanning crowds, I didn't notice the mixed ways audiences applaud. Now, I'm a Handclap Watcher.

Lots raise their hands high above their heads, arms outstretched, to slap open palms together. Try it, it's hard work and resembles a new exercise regimen. The gyrations toggle the shoulders and the procedure is sure to block the view of anyone behind these ceiling beaters.

The flat handed applauders, with five fingers aimed westwardly and five easterly, look childish. With no air being trapped, this method lacks tonal quality. A sort of trilling stutter comes from holding the hands straight and flat up in a prayerful position, locking palms and rocking closed fingers back and forth. Not sound effective but probably restful and painless.

The experienced and demure, execute clapping by cupping the left hand and bouncing four tightly closed fingers of the right hand in and out, briskly, of the readied left hand crevice. Keeping contact distance short allows more slaps per second and relays a deep throated roar, superior to the clicking pitches of the other above mentioned hand driven static procedure.

These days, seldom is heard the encouraging word of "Bravo". Shouts of "Encore, encore," and the informal through-the- teeth whistles have nearly vanished. The piercing, shrill whistles were a source of pride for those able to produce them. Perhaps the work of orthodontists straightening teeth has wrecked the emergence of a new generation of whistlers. That, or fathers are too busy to teach their sons the technique.

Standing ovations are prevalant around our area. That reminds me of the custom of standing during the performance of the "Hallelujah Chorus" in Handel's Messiah. The King was in attendance and jumped to his feet a moment after the music began. Everyone followed suit and for years it's been thought that the King, so moved by the chorus, stood to show his appreciation and reverence. There's also the story afoot that the King got a cramp in his leg and leaped up hoping to ease. Naturally everyone would do as the King did and the custom remains to this day. The reverent reason is plausable no matter what the King experienced.

Actually, I wish we could think of a substitute for applause. It's so noisy and brittle and punctuates, no ruptures, in a split second, the emotional awe yearning to be embraced heart and soul before an outward physical response. Stunned silence would make a positive statement, then a "bravo" or two and finally, thundering applause if we must have it and I guess we must. It's instinctive.

Haven't people with pierced noses heard that pigs are given snout rings to keep them from digging out of their pens and the ring in a bull's nose is a way to control him when a stick lead is hooked to the ring? Women should forego any permanent make-up injections or they'll never be able to "see" how bad they're feeling. Too, when the woman grows old and her skin no longer fits, her resident blush could lop southerly to join the lipline or slide on to decorate her neck waddles.

Cruelty done to a birthday tot is a cake with those blasted candles that won't blow out. Eyes aglow, they puff and nothing happens. They feel foolish and tricked. Guests, young and old, gaffaw and the honored child is dishonored by being unduly embarrassed.

YOU DON'T SAY

"A people's speech is the skin of its culture." (Max Lerner-"America as a Civilization".)

"Each day the human mouth expels so many words that inevitably a percentage will emerge as irrelevant embarrassingly egotistical, meaningless, shocking, inane or just appallingly dumb." (Lewis Grossberger New York Post March 23, 1974.)

"Talking" has become passe. We're now supposed to communicate" or "dialogue". Whatever we call it, gabbing over the back fence is on the wane.

Face to face visiting is no longer the norm. Surely television is partly to blame for this sorry state of mass silence and ensuing loneliness. Haven't you dropped in to visit family or friends and been treated like an intruder because you've interrupted their favorite show? If you're lucky, they'll press "mute" on their remote so you can exchange three sentences during the ads.

Of course, the best policy is to phone before dropping in and it's ideal if they own a VCR so they can watch the show after you've left. Leave early.

A child gave a new slant to the Lord's Prayer with ". .lead us not into temptation and deliver us from E mail.." The computer obsessed find little time to spend with live voices complete with nuances of tone and body movements.

Double job family parents haven't much extra time to converse with their children let alone other adults. Daycare youngsters can't possibly pick up the conversational skills they'd learn if they were home with a talking parent, grandparent, one or two playmates, not a dozen. Speaking and listening gets splintered when either young or old find themselves in a crowd--more than three.

Stay-at-home young adults are, today, hard pressed to find someone free for lunch talk. Their parents may have taken late "hobby" jobs and grandmothers live 359 miles yonder, hate telephones and forget they haven't written lately. The loss of ready sounding boards means missing gems of wisdom shared to the betterment of sanity minus the expense of consulting a psychiatrist or dialing the psychic hotline. It's no help discussing your husband's shortcomings with his mother, the only female within easy visiting distance.

The one sided direction of radio and talk shows can't fill the gab gap. The only service talk shows offer is making you feel you're doing well not leading as decadent a life as the guests relating all the sordid, gruesome details of their woeful lives. You can also rightly feel superior when you hear them say, " I done... I seen. .",and the hosts of other grammatical errors destined to set your teeth on edge. Isn't it strange that one saying, "I seen the firetrucks go by" and hearing in reply, "I, too, saw the trucks go by," isn't a speck curious as to which tense is correct?

Words separate us from animals and fowl, with the exception of parrots and myna birds unware of what they're saying anyway. It's mind boggling that language evolved from grunts and ughs to dictionaries. With the vast amount of words we have, why do we have so many ill-spoken among us? Is it fadish to have a woefully depleted vocabulary littered with vulgarities and murdered grammar or what?

The slipping of speech into the gutter diminishes the attempt to retain what little human dignity we have left. The trend of faulty, sloppy, crummy speech could eventually divide us when those with an excellent command of language will be able to dupe those without. Those left behind won't know what they're signing, voting for, reading or hearing. Thus, those with polished syntax will have the language loafers by their virtual tarnished tongues and stopped up ears.

It's your prerogative to use the current buzz words that frankly, I think, are becoming tiresome. Nobody dies anymore, they pass". Pass a test, gas, kidney stone, bridge hand, a truck? Given our national fixation with staying forever young, death may soon be described as, "living impaired."

Absolutely "absolutely" could benefit from a rest. Often drawn to its outer limits, "ab---soooo-looot-lee" resembles a verbal somersault when a simple, "yes", would do nicely.

Right up there with "absolutely" is, "closure". Putting a "stop" or an "end" to something troublesome carries more force.

Listen and hear batches of the highly educated leaving the "t" out of "important". It's become "impordant" with a "d". Also, many a criminal is now being given a "senence". Where "t" has gone is as curious as where fruit flies come from.

There's been quite enough of, "me and my friend. .all's I got... this is where I am at. .". With ego determined to be first in line, then me and my friends has all's we can endure and you'ns ain't got absolutely no idear where we're at wanting closure to the passing away of the impordance of a good senence. As rushed as many claim to be, for the sake of brevity, "This is where I am", is not only correct but shorter. Please, "My friend and I went skating."

Words are intensely interesting. How people use them equally as intriguing, when not disgusting. As long ago as 600 B.C., Greek philosopher Pythagoras said, " The oldest, shortest words--'yes' and 'no'--are those which require the most thought."

Words continue to go in and out of vogue, as reflected by new dictionaries including words that refuse to budge from the common vernacular. "Ain't", in a 1967 edition, is said to be, "nonstandard, although users of standard English sometimes say or write it for amusing effect when they are sure it won't be taken as their normal usage.

Let's put the "l" back in "vulnerable" and omit the "r" on the end of "Cuba". I heard the man from Kingsville, Texas, lost in his quest to take the "hell" out of "Hello". He wanted people to say, "Heaveno". Perhaps he could try getting the "fun" out of "funeral."

Speech patterns can be entertaining or annoying. A man we know is a phrase repeater: "I decided to go golfing although it was raining. Yeah, I did. I decided to go golfing. I got soaked. I did. I got soaked."

I live with a time lapse talker. Without a hint of reference, Jim is apt to state his closing remarks about something we discussed days ago. Out of the blue comes, "I think she'd have known she couldn't trust him."

"Who's she" Who's he? What are you talking about?"

His sudden plunge back into three day old subject matter is like a postscript minus the letter.

The helper-mumbler, giving voice to every other word you're saying, prods me into trying to out race him so my last word isn't his, too. It's a case of back pedaling that makes talking to him difficult. I'm guilty of filling another's groping pauses to keep the wheels moving. It's a tacky habit.

Let's not disparage small talk. It deserves its place because it promotes civility, may give rise to new ideas and unexpected information that turns into an opportunity. It's a stage upon which to practice the art of making a good impression. The best part of surface chatting with strangers is being able to present the best facets of your personality without argument never having to invite them to dinner.

It's the detail talker who's the most frightening. Remember, when telling a story about finding a toad in your toilet, no one cares what you ate for breakfast, what the weather was or what you were wearing. The fact that your child thought it was a frog and needed to be in water is enough. And, always speak clearly, fuzzed words aren't fertile.

It's not my imagination that I'm hearing more and more people failing to utter a period at the end of a sentence. Instead of dropping the tone, they're lifting it into the question mark range. Oddly disturbing and robot like: "I went to the show? I was lucky to get a front seat?"

Along with the slow death of small talk, big talk, and, reportedly, fewer people reading books, adages are in danger of dying from not being seen or heard.

Many have suffered from being modernized into slogans of dubious content: "Do unto others before they do unto you", a lousy, intentional mistreatment of Scripture is one example. Many worthy sayings are deemed to be old fashioned verbal crutches used by the feeble minded.

Engrossed as we've become in adoring shortcuts and instant results, it's curious that adages, proverbs, platitudes, etc., haven't enjoyed a revival by virtue of their brevity as well as their sense. Like them or not, many represent our heritage coming, as do many, from the Bible, Benjamin Franklin, noted writers, grandparents, philosophers, disciplinarians, et al. Let's not cheat our youth by throwing away these abbreviated truisms meant to encourage good attitudes and behavior.

One gripe, regarding quotations, hinges on those thought to be contradictory: ''He who hesitates is lost'', doesn't support, "Look before you leap". Or does it? Doesn't it depend on the depth of the ditch? The same applies to Bible verses appearing to be in conflict. The differences are wonderful in that, singularly, there's one to apply to every imaginable human situation.

Grandmother rattled off capsuled directives without pause or apology. "Waste not, want not", was a favorite and has stuck to me like glue. I save everything in case I'll need it later. I usually do, if I can find it. Grandma felt waste was sinful and not getting every last mile out of things wasn't being a good steward of one's material blessings.

I so agree that I've been caught washing paper cups, saving string, recyling envelopes, etc., etc. I've not yet sunk to laundering dental floss probably because I've run out of teeth.

Thoreau's, "A man is rich in proportion to what he can do without," is a splendid reason for not bothering to, "Keep up with the Joneses". We're completely stupid if we haven't figured out that an over abundance of "things" becomes, as the Bible says, "burdensome". God knows it takes endless energy and money to keep motorized things oiled and running, inanimate things clean and insured.

As a result of thrifty Grandma's training and a host of relatives reveling in making something out of nothing, I go shopping only when there's desperate need.

"Shop until you drop", strikes me as insane, expensive and torturous. Compulsive shoppers have to be mixed up as to what's want and what's need.

"I really like that but can manage to live without it," I told a clerk about a large, Christmas angel figure holding a candle in her arm that moved back and forth to the accompaniment of electronic carols coming from a recorder in her white velvet chest. Beautiful.

The saleswoman knows me and egged me on. "If you like her, why not treat yourself? You can afford her."

Coining an axiom on the spot, I replied, " Yes, and I can afford her because I'm not going to buy her."

The clerk's face registered bewilderment and I saved $250, as fate would have it, the exact amount of car repairs needed the next day.

Thinking of, "Money as a tool", and having it, "work" for me, I don't fuss over spending on a work implement that's going to improve and increase my earnings. if I need it!

Back to sayings. Running them past youngsters will often instigate an unexpected conversation.

"Out of the frying pan into the fire", or, "Don't look a gift horse in the mouth", are examples of expressions apt to catch a child's attention and curiosity. There's a wealth of opportunity in explaining, "Don't bite the hand that feeds you." I fear the days of, " A child should be seen and not heard", are long gone, but, is sometimes needed.

"A stitch in time saves nine," I told son Matt, intent on pulling apart his half torn pant's pocket.

"Nine what?" he asked, and off I went into the merit of mending capped by, "Don't put off 'til tomorrow what you can do today.

Detrimental to learning and living are the distorted quotes: "Money is the root of all evil", is WRONG, WRONG, WRONG and we hear it all the time. It's "the LOVE of money", which makes it a whole 'nother ballgame.

"Raise up a child in the way he should go and he won't depart from it," is another hatchet job. It should say,"...when he's OLD he won't depart...", doubtless parents of wayward kids would rather not hear how long reform may take.

"Nipped in the butt (bud)" and "Prying (praying) on my mind", are off-center yet do fit certain instances. A councilman vowed an ordinance would be passed. "On my dead body", rather than "over". Nor was he going to take any "slack", instead of "flak"(W.W.II anti-craft fire) over the outcome.

Anxious to investigate school children's knowledge of adages, I circulated sheets of partial adages to fifth graders. Nearly all knew "one good turn deserves another". One thought, "one good turn deserves a push." As for, "It never rains but it pours", many did write, "pours", others wrote: "snows"; "sleets"; "shines". A doozy was, "It never rains but it might."

It was disturbing to read," A penny earned is a penny spent", and worse, "A rolling stone gathers no evidence." Not all was lost on that one, saved by kids who said the stone gathered: "friends"; "rocks"; and, yes, "moss" showed up.

The consensus was, "You'll break a lot of glass if you live in a glass house and throw stones." In case you've forgotten, the early bird catches: "the sun"; "the train", "the egg". The winner was, "Don't give up the ship." Second place was, "Keep your nose to the grindstone." Good!

A postscript to the adage report: Sayings become more believable as one collects years. The old saw, "That makes me sick", said when one is under 40, isn't as factual as when you're older. With each added year, the expression moves into factual mode as does, "That breaks my heart," or, "That drives me crazy. Being "all played out" plays out just as it says.

Senior citizens hear a swarm of new, perky quips. "You're only as old as you feel", is infuriating when hearing this on a day when I feel older than water and meaner than dirt. This catch phrase implies that even a condensed organ recital of my physical woes is inappropriate and stems from a bad attitude. There's not a glimmer of sympathy to tweak out of this reprimand, slathered in silver tongued ignorance. Best to keep silent or become the truth of, "A bore is someone who, when you ask how he is, tells you."

To "grow old gracefully" had to originate out of the mouth of a young person.

The dear advocate asks for a smoother transition than some hanger-oners can muster. Those of us with creeping forgetfulness can't remember the quote let alone regain the aplomb and style so ordered so we aren't living reminders to the young that their day's coming.

"Retire" is an odd word. Does being retired mean you were formerly tired and now you're more tired or that you've gone to bed? "Wear your wrinkles proudly, you've earned them." I resent all my troubles being registered on my face advertising, to the lippy quoter, that I've been dumb enough to have amassed a mess of them.

"The good die young" fills me with foreboding in that I must be bad to have lived so long. "You're not getting older, you re getting better." Often the only thing I'm doing better is getting older. After a day of accommodating a bevy of people with favors and not getting a sniff of one done me, I'm for changing the "getting better" to "getting bitter."

I'm going to give this up or you'll be "fit to fly' and "climbing the walls". I do admit that some old saws are aren't worth their sawdust or "the powder to blow them up." Some are helpful. Some are just right for little scoldings.

Make up a parlor game by abbreviating a known saying using a capital letter only for the beginning of each key word:

H.W.L.L.L.B.-He who laughs last, laughs best.

D.L. a G.H.in the M.-Don't look a gift horse in the mouth.

The P. is M.than the S.-The pen is mightier than the sword.

T.H. are B. than 0.-Two heads are better than one.

Y.C.T.an O.D.N.T.-You can't teach an old dog new tricks.

I.at F.Y.D.S.T.T.A.- If at first you don't succeed, try, try again.

In the mind of a child, the 'succeed' line could be truthfully construed to: "If at first you don't succeed, cry, cry again.

Perchance the expression mind benders become over done, invent a few common knowledge sets:

9 P. in the S.S.- Nine planets in the solar system

13 S. on the A.F.- Thirteen stripes on the American flag.

40 D.and N. of the G.F.-Forty days and nights of the Great Flood.

7 W. of the A.W.- Seven wonders of the Ancient World.

Song and book titles furnish another possible grouping.

Teasing, as opposed to good natured banter("Did you truly break your arm or do you think a cast complements your outfit?") ,is generally not as amusing as it is cruel.

According to the news, kids teasing/taunting kids has reached giant proportions with parents of the meanies and school authorites doing little to stop it.

There's something to be said about cranking up enough courage to pretend the teaser's remarks aren't bothersome--this response often helps. However obnoxious child-to-child, adult-to-adult teasers are, the adult-to-child ones are the pits.

An example of trust-busting teasing:

"Oh, I think your new brother (or puppy) is so cute, I think I'll take him home with me," says the pea-brained grownup, as he or she picks up the baby and heads for the door. This follows have hidden the child's candy bar.

These jokers are the ones who hide a child's favorite toy, claiming they gave it to the kid down the street. Why is any of this supposed to be funny when it srikes terror and a sense of helplessness in the heart of a child?

Have pity on the performing child getting laughed "at" when not trying to be comedic. Stifle those giggles when the tot nervously twists her skirt, the wee chap picks his nose or the muffed lines are rare and side-splitting.

For Pete's sake, when you see Pete for the first time in twenty years, don't stick your hand out and say, "Hi, Pete, remember me?"

Pete doesn't, is mortified to admit his memory loss and embarrassed knowing you're instantly hurt by being so unforgettable.

To spare you both, approach Pete, extend your hand and say, "Hi, Pete, I'm Grace Saving. Nice to see you again'

XO   XO   XO

Be careful using the memory jogging word-image association for connecting names with faces.

Mark deducted that Mrs. Long looked for all the world like a chicken. When she entered his store a week later, he laid an egg by greeting her as Mrs. Leghorn.

0   0   0

My husband, Jim, has trouble talking with anyone speaking with a foreign accent. He reacts by talking very slowly while screaming as if they're deaf.

Much as he knows telephones have improved since 1929, he automatically raises his voice, convinced all callers must be in northern Siberia.

In reverse, son Tim's phone voice is so soft we're forced to beg for volume. He's a good impersonator and doctored many different answering machine welcomes leading us to wonder if we rung the right number.

Three people we know begin telephone conversations with a childish, "Hi, it's me." It's not confusing since each has a recognizable voice. I answer them, "Oh, hello there me."

One friend answers the phone, "Hello, you're looking good. Come in." Different and rather uplifting.

What to do with the halting talker filling blank moments with labored breathing? Breathe back?. Do you just wait through pregnant pauses or rapidly change the subject?

I really want to shake callers refusing to give me a message. "Is Jim there?"

"Yes, he's in the basement printing. Shall I get him?"

Jim doesn't hear me beckon, I run all the way to the cellar to fetch him, he turns off the press, comes upstairs to hear, "Just wanted to remind you of the board meeting tonight."

Jim hasn't forgotten. Secondly, am I not bright enough to relay this momentous proclamation? Even asking for the message doesn't bear fruit from the stubborn, one track minded. My record of message delivering is flawless, superior to Jim's, due to his failing hearing. Darned if he'll admit he doesn't hear something. Oh, no, he makes up what he didn't get and now we're all in the dark. If he doesn't get the caller's name, the mystery deepens and can't be solved by phoning back and starting again.

No one, in person, or on the telephone, should start off with," What are you doing tomorrow afternoon?"

Mercy, what a dilemma this question creates. To reply, "Not a thing,", opens the door for getting stuck with a "doing" you might loathe. By the same token, in a deft maneuver of self-protection, saying, "I'm all tied up," you risk missing a golden opportunity.

If these quizzical folks don't first state the reason they want to know what you're doing tomorrow, your reply needs to be, "What's up?", before you commit to an unknown happening. To know what's planned gives you control over the decision you're to make. Not being told up front is a form of entrapment. It's the ideal time to answer a question with a question.

This leads nicely into a brief assessment of white lies: the bane of the strickly honest person's life. Not to fall into the trap of pesky cover-ups, sidestep by learning to give an answer that's a non-answer. To whit:

Q. "Do you like my new dress?"

A. " It's most unusual. ("different" or "outstanding" also suffice.)

Q. (Mother with new, homely baby) "Isn't he cute?"

A. "He looks so healthy."

This type of "Artful Dodger" answer relieves most situations where the absolute truth would be brutal and serve no purpose. There's always the chance that the sharp listener knows darned well you're skirting the issue. If this is obvious, backtrack some and allude to the niffty collar of that dress, the baby's really cute hands and begin again. As babies go, they're so dear I can't remember ever seeing one who was totally uncute.

Could be that telling a fib, and then setting about to turn it into truth is sinful. However, I did it a few times. "Sorry, we can't accept your invitation because we're planning to have guests that night,"

The next step was to make that come true by hastening to invite people here on that date. This was to keep from being caught lying in flying colors.

The use of "was", I'm happy to confess, means I had guilt pangs about the first lie, which led, as lies do, to the effort involved not to be found out. Having to work so hard being dishonest wasn't worth it. Now, simply decline, softly as possible, all invitations I don't want to accept.

The power and freedom savored by saying, "No", is most remarkable.

"Will you canvass your block for the Such and Such campaign drive?"

No. I'd rather not," without a hint of an excuse. The no excuse baffles the caller more than the blunt turndown. I did tell her I'd done our block for the past 15 years--that's how she knew to call me. Surely it will take another 15 years of saying no before my name goes off her list.

It wouldn't hurt my feelings to never again hear "Boobs" and "Buns". Both are confusing to any of us remembering when "boobs" were numbskulls, hence the television known as a "boob" tube. However, with as many plunging necklines as we see there, perhaps the tube has earned the right to share the word both ways. "Buns" used to be individually shaped mounds of baked bread dough, over consumption of which can expand behinds.

As for "pee" and "poop"--both make me cringe. Spoken by adults crinkles me more than hearing it from children lacking a nicer word through no fault of their own--except that "their own" could surely have taught a more refined something as clear and neat as, "Go to the bathroom." These "P" words rolling out of anyone over 12 ,is childish.

"No use complaining," is a weak, whinning answer to, "How are you?" A snappy, "Can't complain" is okay but not great.

Just look at how the "No use" one's loaded: it's martyrish; implies the questioner hasn't the capacity for sympathy or problem solving; mean, to present a riddle with no answer; selfish to hint at troubles and not recite them so the greeter is relieved hearing his are comparatively less; dumb, for by giving voice to whatever it is there's no use complaining about, the speaker may gain new perspective merely by hearing himself. More chance of this if he keeps the list short and pops in a little laugh here and there.

Honestly, people like to be consulted and be of help. Don't deny them this avenue. Furthermore, free advice can be worth a bundle. Being shy and secretive isn't productive.

Case in point: asked how I was one day I said, "Frantic, I need a clown suit by 2 p.m. for a photo shoot." The person told another person, that person another, and by noon I had the outfit. A headache remedy was another find, etc. etc.

High on the irk list are the rude repartee glances exchanged between the think alikes while another is talking. Versions of eye rollings, lip smirkings, brow and forehead raisings speak unsettling volumes to the speaker noticing these silent, none to subtle, body language assignations. Telepathically, the inferences are more, "Yeah, in a pig's eye". ."Who's she kidding?". ."How tiresome". .than, "Whow, this is interesting."

It's enough to rattle the most entertaining spokesman. Right up there with the glancers are the overlay chatters-two carrying on a side conversation during the main one going on.

And then we have the joke and idea thieves. You tell an innocuous joke to someone beside you. He enjoys it. Moments later, he claims it, saying, "You've got to hear my latest story." Away he goes expecting you to play dumb and laugh along even though he doesn't tell it well.

The parade committee wants a theme for the float. Elsie suggests a good one. Others are heard. Ten minutes later, Jesse rises to her feet. "I've just thought of a dandy one," she says, and proceeds to outline, word for word, exactly what Elsie had proposed. The half-asleep committee doesn't remember it as Elsie's idea and Elsie's too shy to defend herself. Jesse never gets around to crediting Elsie.

Jesse isn't mean. She just mixes up what she's heard with what she thinks she thinks. It's important, however, to give credit where credit's due. Let us not shrink from also rising to our feet to remind everyone, "Yeah, that's precisely what Elsie suggested. Great that you approve of it, Jesse."

Although Jesse may now be muddled and embarrassed, she's been done a favor: made an honest woman; taught that she ought to listen more carefully and, hereafter, champion committee members willing to stand up for the truth and one another.

A fuss about nothing? Picayune? Maybe on the surface but it addresses the matter of character, especially since Jesse pulls public verbal plagiarism regularily.

If you know a Jesse, and you're an idea Elsie, and there's no one around rising to their feet, on the side of justice, call her on the carpet yourself.

And then there's the curse of misguided sympathy.

Example: Tom has just learned he has a serious illness. He tells Ralph (a mistake), whereupon Ralph is quick to impart, "Boy that's a shame. You'd better take good care of yourself. Ya' know, my cousin had the same thing and died in three weeks."(What Tom needs to hear is about Ralph's neighbor successfully beating the disease and still going strong.)

Louise is expecting her first child. Three young mothers and one old one do everything short of drawing diagrams to explain how gruesome her labor will be. All four vie to be the, "Leading Sufferer of the Century".

I was on hand during one of these pain by pain recitations and plunged in to tell the expectant mother how I delivered my first baby in an hour, the second in half an hour and the third in fifteen minutes. She was ecstatic and I was instantly the most unpopular guest at the shower.

The dear girl later followed my instructions of pretending to be a piece of limp liver or black velvet with the pre-pushing pains. On to laboring like one possessed when the immense push and shove contractions mean business. Isn't there a scientic law about matching one force with another of equal power that keeps either from getting the upperhand?

Well anyhow, I gave the woman all these tips and she had her darling boy in two hours. It was then her turn to be the "Wet Blanket" at the next party and shoot down the "Through Hell and Back but Worth It" stories.

Scare mongers deserve our regrets for their ordeals. Never-the-less, I wish they'd can the gory details out of kindness and for the health of their memory banks.

Let's liken this 'dashing of hopes' stuff to letting a child or adult tell you something you already know without admitting it: "Grandma, did you know George Washington was our first President?"

"That's nice to know, dear." This answer doesn't dilute his pleasure and young excitment of sharing.

"Have you heard my good news?," bubbles Debbie.

You suspect you have. "Hurry, tell me, " you enthuse, saving Nancy, Debbie's friend, from blame for having told what was supposed to be a secret. Behave as if newly informed by Debbie and don't top her with your good news saga. Let yours wait a day or two if it's more grand.

"You're dress is pretty."

"This old rag? I've had it ten years," bashes the compliment into a tin hat and infers that the one commenting doesn't recognize pretty from ragged and is nine years late with "pretty" at that.

"I was cleaning house and thought you'd like to have back these photos you gave me," Mary says to Laura.

Better Mary throw them away and not tell. Laura wants Mary to want them or she wouldn't have given them to her.

WHEN YOU THINK ABOUT IT

"Progress is man's ability to complicate simplicity." Thor Heyerdabl-"Fatu.Hiva". 1974

"We're in this together--by ourselves." Lily Tomlin, quoted in New York Times, Sept. 12. 1976

"Everytime the train of history goes around the corner, the thinkers fall off." Attributed to Karl Marx

The change mongers have given us creatures of habit plenty to suffer. Not even the Bible has remained unscathed.

A 1952 revised edition explains:" Revised versions became necessary as the English language grew and changed through the centuries. Moreover, an older and better Greek text than that used for the Authorized version came to light in newly discovered ancient manuscripts."

It's debatable that our language has grown when it sounds and reads as if it's shrunk. Scripture tinkering that messes with verses I memorized ages ago and puts a spin on the meaning futhermore, fries my faith in translators.

The substitution of "Happy' for "Blessed", in updated Beatitudes doesn't make me happy. How does, "Happy are they that mourn: for they shall be comforted.", compare with "Blessed are they that mourn..."? It's reasonable to me that it's a blessing to have the capacity to mourn and another blessing to find God's comfort in grief. "Blessed" has more depth.

With six different editions turning up in Sunday School or Bible study classes, reading Scripture in unison, or reading silently along with the reader, is reminiscent of the song, "Let's Call the Whole Thing Off": "I say pajamas and you say pajawmas", etc. One person's saying "Thine", another "Yours". Whole sentences become mismatched and it's an audible mish-mash.

If such modifications are to enable poor readers to better understand the Bible, the merit includes the danger that such enabling will create waves of yet poorer readers. What's so taxing about learning that a "tare" is a "weed'? Simplify the King James Biblical vocabulary much more and we'll end up with little more than, "See Jane. See Jane run." In that event, there would arise a sexist objection and a concerted effort to neuter Jane, Dick and Spot to mere people and a dog. (A cleric says I'm wrong to complain because the new translations are more accurate. Oh? Right or wrong, the poetic beauty and literary flow added more majesty than do the new versions.)

It gives one pause as to why God as a Father is so reprehensible in these times when so many fathers have removed themselves from their families for whatever reason. You'd think having God as the epitome of a Perfect Father could, should and would be a source of comfort in place of the loneliness and mistrust foisted on those comparing Him to faulty, earthly fathers.

Add the campaign to degender God and the blurring increases. Tacking all these neutering names to God--he, she, it, person--seems insubordinate and has elements of divisiveness.

The Bible sanitizers march onward without, in many churches, "Christian Soldiers"--those of the once favorite hymn. Waging war against the gates of Hell with the "Cross of Jesus going on before.." is a disagreeable stance? If we could

46

win the war addressed in this hymn, there'd be less trouble of man against man--oops, person against person. The message and the music of that hymn are missed.

Playing a large, fine organ for enthusiastic hymn singers is a joy. Being paid to do so doubles the joy. However, it isn't always without incident.

I've been known to lose my place in the number of verses sung when a hymn has a repetitive chorus or refrain. Either I lop off a verse or play the last one twice. My thanks to singers who've memorized the chorus and audibly snap their books shut as a clue to me that the last verse has been sung.

A classic mix-up occured one Christmas Eve with the church packed and people eager to sing carols. The choir has sung beautifully and the organ had behaved-no notes going unconscious or screaming non-stop. Not a hitch until after my introduction to, "Hark! the Herald Angels Sing." To my dismay, no one began singing. After a few more measures and still no voices heard, I stopped for a split second and began anew. Nothing.

Frantic, I plunged on and eyed the bulletin and raised eyebrows in the direction of the choir. At last, Nate, in the tenor section, sped to my side and hissed, "What are you playing, mother?" (Nate has moments of wondering if I was born just to embarrass him.)

"I'm playing 'Hark'. Why isn't anyone singing?"

"Because you're playing, 'Christ the Lord Has Risen Today', muttered Nate, mortified and unsympathetically.

"I am not!" I shot back. "Look at the title."

Not easily rattled, knowing no one's perfect and remembering Kit saying never flinch, shrug or indicate you've made mistakes, I stopped playing, looked at the minister and asked, "What's happened?"

He smiled and didn't offer a a word. Not to be done in, I grabbed the hymnal and turned the page. Sure enough there was "Hark" again, this second tune being the one everyone knew. I took it upon myself to ask all to turn over the page and they sang boisterously.

The minister hadn't tumbled to the fact that the "Christ the Lord.." music had the "Hark!" lyric. Having played both hymns hundreds of times, I didn't notice the tune change ahead of time either. By the way, customarily ministers to select the hymns. This suits me and gets me off the hook when the congregation dislikes certain ones chosen.

I confess to having made my share of errors--some I couldn't blame on the organ or the choir. Choirs, by the way, are the most wonderful bunch of people. Directors love them they love the director and one another--that's at least been my glorious experience. They get and give extra religiosity by virtue of the music they

47

prepare and sing.

After another memorable Christmas Eve service that was a disaster from beginning to end--choir members late, bell choir kids dropped bells a'clanging, I forgot my organ glasses and nearly strangled for the whole hour, the first ending of the anthem skipped, not enough chairs in the choir loft, the minister forgetting to have the offering taken and the town fire siren going off and ten men racing out of the church, three notes on the organ going dead--the preacher later asked, "Was that as bad as I think it was?"

"Compared to what?" I laughed, adding, "Our professions require us to declare even an unholy mess a raving success when we tried to do our best. The effort alone pleases God, I hope."

While this was going on at the Methodist Church, the Presbyterians had a fiasco to end all fiascos. A confused woman, partaking in the intinction Communion, put the bread in her mouth before dipping it into the chalice. Realizing her mistake, she fished the now slimy tidbit out of her mouth and dunked it ever so carefully. Don't you wonder how the next in line managed to take part without a shudder?

One Sunday there was a influx of wasps merrily flitting above heads and perching on the organ keys. One choir rehearsel night, a bat swooped in and dove into one of the exposed organ pipes. We fled. Two years later, the organ repair man found its flattened, leathery carcass at the bottom of that pipe.

There's no end to the stories church musicians can tell. Not to bore you silly, I'll save the rest of mine for another day.

A newspaper article reported church attendance on the increase in churches adding drama, Christain rock music, casual dress, dance, (what have you) to their services. In other words, entertainment.

This distresses my thinking that church should be a spiritual, unworldly, quiet, prayerful, dignified, climbing out of yourself time. How do you interact with God amid such busy distractions? The world whirls us up and around so madly that being in the sanctity of a calming church hour should be appealing for its rest and renewal properties, compared to the clamor of everyday life. Church is an opportunity to shut out the world for a time, not drag it in with banners waving.

Makes me wonder if sending youngsters off to "playtime church", started a generation ago in many churches, has those children, now adults, determined to keep the "play" in their church time. If that's the case, it was a large foozle.

It's a rare child, four or older, who can't sit still and quiet during church--or be bribed or threatened into it. Being there, they learn the hymns and other responses. They may think they hate it but,". .when he's old, he'll not depart from it."

If Play Church isn't to blame, let's credit the demise of the Blue Laws. If you're too young to know about these, they kept stores, bars, and most everything else

48

closed on Sundays. Church was the place to be, something to do and the day of rest had no competition. Forced or not, it worked.

Restaurants should shred those yard high menus. The darned things are dangerous: opened carelessly they could behead the person across from you. Nor can people wearing bifocals ever read the top lists of offerings without inserting the bottom part of this hard plastic coated document mid-abdomen. I've debated setting such sky scraper menus on the floor to double as a temporary coat hanger.

As for place mats: those with triva questions need turned upside down to get the answers; the puzzle ones don't come with a pencil; the center section's Fair event schedule is covered by your plate before you can memorize it; Jim's prelude to the meal is ranting about bad spelling and awkward letter and/or line spacing in the border ads.

As for the tableware: Knife, fork and spoon are delivered bound by a sticky paper ring strong enough to keep a truck load of steel pipes from slipping; after breaking a fingernail fighting it loose, therein is one of those fool, long, two-pronged forks more a weapon than a dining utensil. These swords probably promote graceful movements getting food to mouth without injury. It's also probable that the time they consume to consume, in mannerly fashion, lengthens customer waiting lines to delay seatings and thus, reduces profits and tips.

The buffet itself: hot salad plates limp the lettuce and thin dressings; advance self-servers have glopped up various selections with bits and pieces of neighboring ones. Partly, the messy fallout is due to those food scoops large enough to hold a cubic foot of top soil but unable to grasp and contain a single, black olive. It sucks up four, two of which scoot out into the nearby cottage cheese. Mushrooms dotting the pudding is lip curling.

Ashtrays: amazing how many smoking area table setters forget to place the ashtray and look surprised when asked for one.

The check: If in a hurry and not wanting dessert, ask for the check the moment you receive food. Waiting half an hour to locate the waitress and another 15-minutes to get it, interferes with smooth disgesting.

Do you suppose the reason most all stores now stay open all day Sunday is because store loyalty has vanished and the owners daren't chance fickle customers discovering the competition?

What a terrific waste of postage caused by computers whisking out "unpaid" notices for bills paid three months ago and three weeks ahead of the due date to boot. Is the loss corrected by raising prices or firing the procrastinating filers? I think we know. It's evident when we renew a magazine three months before it runs out and get two copies per month for three months. That stunt really costs them and me too, if they scramble their records and don't supply three free copies at the end of this newest deal.

If ever turkeys disappear from Thanksgiving tables, blame the bird butchers who hammer in those impossible-to-remove wire hickeys to keep the drumsticks from flopping around.

These turkey turkey fixers lack compassion for cooks and time wasted fighting that bracket gadget. It's a rare woman with strength enough to rock, pull, tug, yank or saw it loose to get the giblets out and the stuffing in. Short of borrowing the fire department's 'jaws of life', how does a lone woman cope with this job?, I thought, as I woke Jim to come to my culinary rescue.

He, armed with the pilers, having done me no good except to gouge and chew up the fowl's flesh, staged his attack in earnest and with blood in his eye. (The blood reference not an idle phrase when exertion of this magnitude tends to dislodge eyeballs.)

Jim struggled, wrenched and tried wire cutters before going after the hacksaw. Aiming the saw's long blade, enlightened my noble wire puller to the fact that splitting the bird's breatbone and nicking the counter top would be part of this operation.

"Let's put the turkey on a towel on the floor. I'll hold it down while you put a towel wrapped foot on it and pull. That'll give you lots of leverage," I said.

"Yeah, and if it suddenly gives way, I'll be smacked up against the ice box."(a term used for its brevity.)

"Well, get your back against it to begin with and then when the wire lets go, you'll only knock your fists into your mouth."

Jim frowned. Back to the pliers. He woggled the wire again before suggesting, "If we partially cook this beast, that wire will fall right out."

"Meanwhile, the giblet's paper bag melts and gums up the insides and I'll have to wear asbestos gloves to put in the stuffing."

Heaven sent, Matt strode into the kitchen. Five inches taller and heavier than Jim, he assessed the truss busting situation and said, "Here let me do that."

Like magic, one draggle with the pliers and the stubborn metal configuration jumped into his hand. Thrilled, I still hate when that happens. You know, you battle to the death a contrary can lid only to have a weakling unscrew it without running it under more hot water, beating it with a knife handle or working up a single bead of sweat. I swear it's because the real work has already been done but the show-off never believes that. Jim was mortified. "You just squeese the wire and then pull," Matt instructed, for further reference.

Anyway, I'm going to write the packing house responsible for our two annual fits over these embedded horrors. Can't they come up with a lovely rope tied in a bow so frail ladies can get dinner going without a block and tackle?

For every telemarketer ruining dinner, waking the baby, detaining a bathroom stop just to hawk something you want about as much as middle-age acne, have fun with the one of twenty catching you with time to spare.

Seriously, if an English speaking sales person isn't rattling through a written spiel, take the opportunity to jump in and sharpen your combative verbal skills.

The DRY BASEMENT GUY: Whether true or not, say you adore your damp, mold-clumping, puddling cellar because the humidity juices your allergy-dry nasal membranes.

As for the seepage crumbling the house's foundation, return the idea that you're 85 and the soggy walls will outlive you six ways to Christmas.

The STORM WINDOW PAIN: Point out how desirable it is to have 24 floor-to-ceiling windows leaking like lace buckets. Tell him, or her, it's wonderful to have these all emitting drafts of health-giving ventilation to offset the murderous fumes leeching from carpets, furniture and hateful cigarettes. And, yes, you can afford the herculean heating bills compared to what it would cost to install his storms.

The WOMAN HATER WHO HANGS UP UNLESS ABLE TO SPEAK TO THE MAN OF THE HOUSE: Before pretending you'll summom your male counterpart, ask his company's name and address so you can call the president and inform him his bigoted employee is rude and not smart. Ask, "Don't you know women control most of this country's spendable money?" Stress, "There's no way I'd buy your stuff, even if I wanted it, from an outfit allowing salespeople to hang up without a compensatory, 'bye now."

You might try, "Is there a woman in your office with whom I could speak?" If he answers, "No", hang up with a mighty bang. If he say, "Yes", enlist her to add her two cents to your tantrum.

These are alternatives to best the pests when, "I'm not interested," or, "Please remove me from your calling list," is fruitless. When I really have time for this useless banter, I find it amusing especially when the salesman sees the fun and claims it added a new dimension to his day.

The travel folk are dumbfounded when I tell them I don't want to accept my winning trip, for which I must shell out $200 up front. "I hate to travel, Can't think of anything worse when a trip upstairs represents a major journey." This is actual truth, I don't like traveling.

Addicted travelers can't understand my aversion to traveling. They expound about the glory of getting away, the mind broadening opportunities and being exposed to the many other wonders that brighten one's life.

My clipped response remains as constant as my staying home: why spend the money when beautifully photographed travel videos can whisk me away while I'm simultaneously proffered by familiar toilet seat, bed pillow, sanitary, well cooked foods that accomodate my teeth and digestion. I know the language and, if I get lost, someone who knows me can lead me home.

The list includes not wanting to return from a trip to spend two weeks reading piled up mail, scouring the crawling critters out of the refrigerator, unpacking and doing a huge washing.

I end with the fact that I like what I'm doing here and now. I can't drag along the piano, organ, dollhouses, typewriter and iced tea by the gallon through airports and onto cruise ships. The underlying impetus to stay put is knowing our grandchildren can't possibly get along without us for more than three days.

I rather suspect that my early near-sighedness has some bearing on my non-desire to roam .For the years I couldn't see, the home front was shrouded in dense fog but I got used to it. A strange place was a fright. Being in a hotel lobby and not able to see the staircase or swimming with no shoreline visible, gives the feeling of being out of one's element and out of control. Vulnerable.

My arguments usually go over like a pregnant polevaulter. But not to worry. Travelers can wander about, go broke, get dysentery while I sit safe, warm, snug, solvent and healthy in my cloistral nest. All that's left out of the travel videos is the odor of the far flung places. I doubt this is a devastating loss even when they'd be sweet. I'm allergic to the scent of perfume.

Why do human beings who hate to exercise want it to extend their life for five more years if that five years will be filled with more loathsome exercising?

How can anyone know an extra five years of life will be derived from eating this or that, by not eating this or that, by doing or not doing any particular thing unless one is given the privilege of living twice and trying it both ways?

Shoelace makers have gone off the deep end with the new round, slippery shoe strings that don't stay tied. Bring back the old, flat, unshiny, rough ones, please.

I'm sick and tired of dashing from store to store seeking the old, safe kinds for our little ones romping about on asphalt playgrounds destined to step on the untied lopping things, fall and crack their heads. Coming in new shoes are strings so over-long that even when electing to stay tied the bows slop over onto the floor.

Technology is amazing and we can't retain anything as serviceable and ordinary as a good shoestring?

It's not that old dogs can't learn new tricks as why expend the energy when the old tricks work as well or better?

Our dishwasher's now a storage bin because: scraping, rinsing, bending to nestle the now half washed dishes into the yawning, non-fitting slots takes longer than washing the dishes by hand; hand washing eliminates the worry about the dishwasher soap's warning to "keep it out of the hands of children". It's okay then to ingest the residue that clings to the washed dishes?; hand doing does away with the second set of stoopings to unload the dishwasher and finding six pieces stuck with goop the machine missed but heated into petrification; I hear that new dishwashers aren't noisy but we sure heard ours to the exclusion of the seven o'clock news and sparkling conversation.

Hand dishwashing cleans fingernails and soothes stiff finger joints, unless the cook pots are over heavy. The process warms up cold oldsters-as in chilly. When family members grab a towel, companionship comes into play. Also, there's the chance of suckering them into hanging around long enough to do up the seldom used dishes gathering dust in near-by cupboards.

Guests seeing our defunct dishwasher think it's operable. It's best not to tell them differently. It relieves them of guilt when I tell them, " I'd rather we all go into the living room and talk. Let's forget the dishes."

There's no longer a need to change into play clothes, after church or work togs when now it's fashionable to start out in them in the first place.

Why don't we mandate an annual, national, "No Deodorant Week", and then, once and for all, we'd know who's working and who isn't?

How scary wanting to "vote the bums out of office" when their opponents are just as bad or worse.

Verse two: Cross filing candidates have a nerve not to declare their party. These sly, fence sitters are political hermaphrodites.

Automobile running boards were wide enough to stand on while smoothing the backside of one's dress prior to gracefully seating one's self within the vehicle.

These days, it's a duck, dive, pull a hamstring, split your skirt operation along with landing on a seat belt buckle that oddly managed to sneak out of the seat cushion crevice.

All this is set to canned, monotone orders demanding you shut the door and lace your here-to-fore unwrinkled clothes and free breathing mid-section to the confined clutches of the maze of straps, reluctant to stretch as needed. This battle is waged anew upon discovering that being belted puts you out of reach of the radio dials. It's then unbelt, dial, belt; unbelt, dial, buckle up. No wonder tape players are popular. Strain to check out the contents of the backseat and it's unhook again or be choked by the shoulder harness.

The glove compartment in many new cars is so small it barely holds the thumb of one mitten. Rounded dashboard ledge edges send comb, map, pencil and sun glasses, resting thereon, tumbling at the turn of the first corner. I sit short so all I see when backing up the car is the headrest upholstery.

To get into a van, the assistance of a fork lift or a crane would help. Kneepads and a helmet would get one through the tunnel to the back seats more safely. To disembark, a parachute is required, unless you thrill to teetering on the narrow step affair (with your foot turned uncomfortably sideways) while contemplating plunging into space head first.

Those tricky little fin-shaped window vents in the front doors have vanished into thin air. They were great to let air in without wrecking the hair-dos of those in the backseats and stirring up sinus infections.

Someone has run off with car eave spouts. Now, when I de-car after a storm I get hit with a hat full of roof rain.

Putting small and frail people in the back seat away from murderous air bags is nigh impossible when passangers include two kids and two grandmothers. Child car seats are more than I can gracefully maneuver: I can get the tot buckled in but not unfastened short of four trys. Then too, the seats ride so low little eyes see only the back of the front seat and not a whiff of outside scenery. This makes them restless. About the time they fall asleep from boredom, Jim, who's driving, shouts, "Hey guys, look at those horses over there."

Among the life saving additions and money saving subtractions to automobiles, modern defrosters are to be cherished. It's a progressive nice not having to press a bare hand palm against an ice cloaked windshield to form a see through peephole. Backup lights are an improvement if I could see beyond the headrest and figure out how to raise the seat so I could. Good are tires that go flat slowly.

Yard sales unsettle me. An over abundance of wares, many unopened with the original price showing, screams of the vender's unwise spending since the stuff wasn't used.

Along with sellers trying to get nickles for what should be given away to the needy, are the buyers bragging about how they fleeced a seller.

"I got these baseball cards for $2.00 and know darned well they're worth

$150.00," giggles the jubilant collector.

The buyer should be ashamed not to have offered the uniformed seller more. Okay, so the seller should get informed ahead of time. That's tough if you're old, tired, and haven't a clue of how to research 500 items. I mean, let's face it, there are bargains to be had and then there's outright theft.

There's the awful of yard sales, like estate auctions, of strangers racking through personal possessions. It's a gross and unnecessary invasion of privacy not unlike airing your dirty laundry in public and coming under the scrutiny of nibby neighbors. Plop the stuff into cartons and get it to the organizations serving the needy. Saves the yard, pricing the things, standing guard all day, finding sacks and tables, haggling with tight wads, covering things if it rains and picking up twenty five pieces that the wind blew into the next county.

It's a curse not to be taken seriously when one is being serious. I have a terrible time convincing whomever I need to convincingly convince. Maybe it's because of my childish voice tone rattling away at breakneck speed coupled with my tendency to be flippant and glib--silly, is more like it.

"So, how's everything at this table?", quizzed a cheery waitress.

"Not so hot. Meaning it's lukewarm," I explained

"That's too bad," she answered and began walking away.

"Will you take this back and reheat it?"

"Oh! I suppose so," the server debates.

She tipped the plate, as she patronizingly snatched it, sending tepid green beans skating into my lap. I draped them back onto the plate and off she went without so much as, "I'm sorry, clumsy of me."

Fellow diners had finished eating by the time my food reappeared registering near 212 degress, if bubbling gravy is any indication of the temperature. Swiping an ice cube through all wasn't an option since our iced teas were icy.

Not wishing others to die of old age waiting for my meal to be eaten safely, I asked for the fiery victuals, hardly palatable from conception, to be boxed for transportation home. Generous ole Jim left a larger tip that I would have, being rather out of sorts by this time.

"Was everything okay?, asked the check-out guy, also the manager.

"No, not really. My meal was too cold and then too hot. To tell the truth, what little I did ingest tasted like fried dust. I'm telling you this because I think it's better for you to know this than have me go out into the world and bad mouth this eating house'

He never flinched a flinch. Instead I got, "Ha, ha, heh, heh", and not a "sorry" in the carload.

55

Let that be lesson unto me of the folly of fiddling with words instead of pounding on the counter, demanding Jim's money back and cramming the food parcel, a poor excuse for sustenance, down his manager-boasting name tag. It was doubltless the fried dust reference that sent him into snickering spasms up, down, across and through his obese torso, clad in a hideous flowery shirt, in order for him to sluff off my complaint.

Things we should invent: slip covers for shoes; see-through, flesh color arm stockings girdles to hide wrinkled, flopping arm skin so one could wear short sleeves without exposing, wiggling, mushing skin; a disposable glove for salad bar eaters to eliminate picking up the collected germs left on the tong handles by everyone serving themselves before you.

Also, cloth newspapers so readers turning pages don't obliterate conversation or one's ability to hear the end of the television movie; We need a sucker-upper gadget at restaurant tables to carry off those contrary cracker wrappers and empty sugar packets; masks and gloves to don when entering a doctor's office waiting room laden with germs from all the other sick people waiting. If there were separate waiting rooms for those with the same ailments, we wouldn't need the masks and gloves.

Mothers would benefit from a kitchen knife with two retractable blades for use by men and teens. One blade scoops jam from the jar, is retracted. The second blade is popped out to spread the jam over the buttered bread. This utensil would put an end to the jam jar being strewn with bits of butter and bread crumbs. Setter yet would be prophylactic lip guards for milk cartons for all the "direct-from-the-bottle-or-carton guzzlers.

Hand clap toilet seat controls to raise and lower the seat along with window opening and closing things, would be a boon. On second thought, combined with clap-on lamps these might be a detriment. Imagine, a car backfires, up goes the toilet seat (hopefully without you on it), the lights go out and a swat of frigid air blasts in from the opened window.

Housework is faster and easier when you learn to do two things at once: straighten the lamp shade and kick the footstool into place at the same time; boil carrots and potatoes in the same pan; dust everything dusty as you pass by it using your shirt tail, hand, or the tissue in your pocket; lean over and finger-sweep the foreign bodies squatting on the carpet; make neat piles of anything sitting askew; stuff back in whatever's dripping from a drawer or leaking out a cupboard or closet door.

Put left-overs into the refrigerator in their cooking pans. Saves dishwashing and

56

food wasted if transferring it from dish to pan later. Don't allow visitors to see this procedure and do use the saved morsels before they discolor the pan, themselves, and/or congeal into immoveable concrete, or worse, begin to sprout bumps of some sort.

Boil the dish rag every other day; Make half the bed before you get out of it; get a long enough telephone cord to enable you to work while talking; wad up the newspaper and toss it at ceiling cobwebs.

Ladies, buy clothes with lots of pockets and never again drag a purse around. Men don't carry pocketbooks so why should we? It glorious freedom to have freed hands and shoulders aligned. You'll walk faster, avoid purse snatchers, never get a purse handle hung up on a doorknob or have to retrace your steps to find where you left it. You'll never have to stand in the soaking rain while you fish in your bag for the car keys beneath 30 pieces of junk you haven't needed in the last ten years you've dragged them along.

Poke into pockets lipstick, comb, keys and loose change. Bills can either go into a thin wallet for a pocket or it can be tucked into your bra. You may bulge oddly here and there but you'll love traveling light and carefree. Stick a tissue over the change rattling about in its pocket to keep it from falling out when you visit the restroom. The tissue also muffles the clangings of coins so you don't jingle as you mingle. Fanny packs aren't for me either. Truly, I've all I can manage to tighten my tummy muscles taut without adding the weight and bulk of an ugly pack that looks for all the world like a inoperable tumor.

Watch and wonder who's been teaching our children how to grip a pencil or pen. The current clutch reminds one of a child grasping a fat crayon. Gone is the index finger aimed down the pencil shaft above a half-curled thumb. It looks weird and awkward. The fist hold also covers up the words one has just written. That has to impede to the whole process.

Have you ever accepted an invitation and said, "Now, please don't fuss,"? Then been miffed because they didn't?

Yes, coffee and tea do taste better when sipped from a thin lipped cup. A doctor claims human lips can readily attach to the fragile rim, shutting out intruding air. Thus, the liquid makes early contact with one's frontal taste buds that doesn't happen when sloshing inward from a heavy bodied mug or cup.

To whom do we turn to have head tables abolished? At the grand affair the honored are seated at a head table where they're stranded and isolated with no one across from them to talk to. Trying to eat and chat with someone beside you makes for missing your mouth and crooked swallowing.

These headers are fed first but they're also finished first with nothing to do but wait in solitary confinement and wonder what the heck everybody's laughing about at the cozy table on their far left.

TELL ME WHY:

Why can't menopausal women have hot flashes when they need them--like walking in the snow?

Why does my hair look its best when I'm combing it out right before I go to bed?

How come store owners don't realize that no clerks or invisible ones keep me from finding things and spending my money?

Why does an innocent person object to having his house searched, blood tested, or whatever else investigated, if he's innocent? Oh! Maybe because they think they can't trust the investigators?

Why does an air conditioned place have to be kept colder in summer than it ever was in winter? Having to clap on a hat, mittens and a coat to traverse the grocery store in July is plain nonsense. Phooey on the store's theory that it keeps the lettuce crisp. I don't stay long enough to find out.

I wait all the northern winter to greet summer's warmth only to freeze in concert halls and restaurants. That isn't mentioning the overhead air vents socking down waffs of the cold stuff to rile the otherwise summer relieved sinsuses. It's misery even with a sweater draped over my head.

Why do we pat a baby, a head, a back, and pet a pet? I pat a pet. You can to, if you want to.

Why do television news people continue to smile when reporting a heartbreaking happening? It strikes me as vain and hard hearted. They ought to wise up and furrow their brows. They probably paid a lot to have their teeth capped.

The, "how do you feel?" questions they impose on someone in shock and so desperately sad is as dumb as it is insulting. Equally as stupid is giving directions of how the thief got into a house, stole a car, made a bomb. Are they nuts? There ought to be a law.

We're constantly told, "You can't legislate morality." Why not? Most of our laws are meant to deter rotten behavior. Censorship is a no-no, yet, in a way, an innocuous stop sign is a form of censorship. I remember the days of movies and books being censored and it nursed a much more polite and civil atmosphere. The freedom for free speech is rapidly becoming freedumb on all four feet.

Why the trend to forego curtains in a house? Is it a way to fool the UPS man, bill collectors, unwanted visitors by making the place look vacant?

Albeit one can see out easier, the world can also look in easier. Do non-curtain hangers relish seeing woodwork chopping up the room in naked, frame-like sections that curtains would normally hide or soften? Do they welcome the noise that clatters about without curtains or drapes to absorb it? What about the furniture getting faded and sunburned?

The fad may be related to getting back to nature, having dust allergies, hating the bother it is to keep window trimmings clean or maybe the cat climbs them. That must be it.

Why don't we wear our clothes wrong side out, underwear at least, so the seams don't rub against our skin?

Why the demise of women in hats? A lady in a grand hat is a lady to be remembered, if only for her hat Hats cover stubborn hair, keep in body heat in cold weather and the sun out in hot weather. Hats create a personal signature and jazz up the plain woman's appearance.

Health wise, a knit cap may do its duty but dragged over ears and forehead and sporting forty dozen grubby fuzz balls doesn't a fashion statement make as does an elegant, glamorous fedora. Even a small, perky hat generates a certain air of flare.

Except for equal pay for equal work, a woman wanting to flail about in the man's role is misguided and soon tired out. I have no burning desire to tote and heave cement blocks and end up with my uterus in my socks.

I'll do my woman's work with dispatch and ability and applaud how delicious and resful it is not to compete.

Why isn't someone appointed to teach kissing? Away with the gruesome, slobbering, open mouth, tongue twitching, cannibalistic, unromantic, slimy, gobbling, face contorting, disease laden kisses that are stomach turners for those of us taught to keep our mouths shut.

Why a Mason jar doubling as a drinking glass? It defies solid lip suction action with dribbles down one's front as the obvious result. The clumsy receptacle is a wrist breaker to lift. Since I want iced tea in hefty draughts, not sips, the straw solution isn't for me. Straw pulling adds a multitude of upper lip puckering wrinkles to the conglomerate amount I foster by my habit of whistling so much.

Much as it's a ego raiser to pretend getting the huge company dinner was no trouble, it's self defeating in the long run. Although you work fast and well doesn't mean you don't work hard, in fact harder than the putterer because good organization, step saving, and deployment thereof, includes brain work, a factor not always factored in by outsiders.

What you must never do is let anyone but immediate family see you in motion as such. Make the grave error of being observed by the general population and you'll be the one assigned to bake seven pies for the next club dinner while the less efficient will bring the olives.

There's free lance organization and then there's big dumb organized rigidity.

Free lance is organizing routine methods of getting a certain job done quickly and well when a certain job needs done. Rigidity is washing the windows every fourth Monday when the windows aren't dirty and it's raining. It's serving chicken every Tuesday night, beef Wednesday, soup Thursday, etc. Away goes imaginative use of left overs and buying foods on sale (waste), never satisfying momentary cravings or serving grand surprises. (Boring.)

Small stupids extend to the fetish for a daily bath whether or not the body needs one. (Time, water and soap consuming and skin drying). Daily changing of unsoiled clothes for different, clean ones. (Wears out the washing machine).

Big dumbs include too many secret telling books being written and other stories with sad endings. We don't need either since we have the evening news dishing out more realism than anyone wishes to assimilate.

A parade big dumb is the ear-splitting, baby waking, sorrowful and fright inducing siren screams and electronic burpings of the parading fire trucks and ambulances.

Why doesn't some cosmetic company come up with sets of face fitting transfers loaded with make-up designed, in advance, to fit your face and coloring. Press this against your face, give it a rub or two and your make-up in on and correctly so in a moment.

These face aides would have corresponding sets of ointment laden ones for equally as fast make-up removal.

I'd find these a glory for, when I apply make-up in a hurry or in the wrong light I look like a case of early Hallowe'en. Because of time and error, I go about the house wearing my customary Normal Anemic.

*   *

Why couldn't we have been born with light weight, no decaying stainless steel teeth insulated against conducting hot and cold?

Also helpful would be infants born with iron filings in their little bottoms. Then, all parents would have to do to reclaim a straying toddler would be to point a powerful magnet in their direction.

++   ++

It's dumb and stupid in whatever amount it irks an adopted person of any age to be introduced or appear in an obituary as, "SoinSo's 'adopted' child." People don't run about saying, "Meet Sally, Molly's real birth child."!

I taught piano 45 years and still wonder why many pianists drape their bodies and swoop their hands and arms all over the place while playing. A hand reaching for the ceiling may imply the performer is "into the music". However, it's more like he's momentarily up and away from it.

Superfluous air swiping and body bobbing strikes me as pure affectation that distracts from the music. Executing a drop roll to beautify phrasing needn't have the elbow rising to ear level. Sit still and play the blasted piece and omit the calisthenics. Pianists who mutter and gargle throughout their performance might better play an instrument that has a mouth piece. I discouraged such antics.

Aren't predictions the wildest things? Warned that you'll be killed traveling to Aunt Lou's tomorrow means you must go and be killed to prove the prediction. When you don't take the plane that's predicted to crash and it doesn't, might it have had you been on it? Perhaps there needs to be a prediction for a prediction.

Because we're advised that most of what we worry about doesn't happen, isn't it then reasonable to nurse a long list of possible horrors to allow the theory to work?

Being taken for granted is a compliment of sorts; it proves how capable and trustworthy you are.

If I hear anymore freaky, messy looking people insisting, "It doesn't matter what I look like on the outside, it's what's on the inside that counts," I'm going to

61

summon the white coated funny farm workers and have them carried off.

Explain please, why anyone so pretty on the inside wants the outside to look as ugly as possible? Any old day I'll give a hoot about trying to discover one's internal beauty when presented with external garbage too high and tiring to hurdle.

Most right handers stick name tags on their left sides. By sticking it on the upper right side, then tag wearers, during hand shaking, don't have to scan the upper torso and bosom to get to the name; eyes travel straight up the arms of the clutching hands without being diverted. It works.

This established, never offer limp, lifeless, dead fish, empty rubber glove, spineless, boneless fade-away handshakes suggesting you're ill, hate people, fear germs and lack ego. Maiming bone crushers are mean. Medium firm is the ticket. Weird how an insipid shake can stay so dead when thrust into a solid shake. Frankly, I'd never hire the shaker that refuses to meet strength with strength.

Pastoring a church is a lonely job. Like the musicians needing a hug because they never get to dance, the minister and family need invitations to dinner, a party, a concert and whatever social things members of the flock do.

Don't be laboring under the opinion that you can't be yourself with a preacher in tow. If your normal self is crude and crass, then you'd better put on a better front. Mostly, pastors want their hosts to act natural and not be on edge or then the minister is destined to apologize for living his or her calling and messing up your evening.

The best reason to be an anonymous giver is not to obligate the receiver on your behalf. If you're paid back, you've had your gift sort of canceled out. It's also safeguard, in case the object of your generosity thinks your a soft touch and makes a habit of expecting handouts.

Aren't you driven crazy by people making God the scapegoat for anything unpleasant that happens?

"It was God's will that I was out of town when the tornado hit and my neighbor was hurt."

How can anyone think that, let alone have the ego and nerve to say it? What does this say about the neighbor? He wasn't worthy to be put somewhere else when the wind blew?

"It was God's will that my son was killed in the war," says the parent, who should know blamed well men make wars, men kill each other. It's human decisions that get us into trouble.

After scolding a "groan" son of ours about his neglect to replace a faulty doorlock, the moment I phoned him another day about un unrelated topic, he answered, "Hi mom, now what am I doing wrong?"

Based on the saying, "What you don't know, won't hurt you", I replied, "What I don't know, won't hurt you until I find out, that is."

Tell me why medical people keep telling us that getting cold doesn't cause us to catch a cold? Chilled or wind blown about twenty minutes and the energy spent shivering sends my normal resistance plummeting, to the awakening joy of the cold bugs, resting, lo these many months, in my nose, throat, ears, sinuses, lungs, and other parts, awaiting their dirty work to do.

Doctors also pooh-pooh that teething makes a baby sick. Well, it does, ask any mother. Maybe it's the slobbering soaking their little chests, not eating because it hurts, not sleeping because of the pain and not to discount the fevered gums that heat up their entire, sweet, tiny faces.

Maybe all retired people, claiming to be busier than when they were working is because now it takes twice as long to get things done.

I don't agree with myself watching Jim chasing around doing favors for family and friends all of whom think they're the only ones enlisting his free time.

It's hard to imagine anyone resting in a "rest" room. However, a waiting room runs true to its name.

Hair combing lessons are in order for mothers racking through a child's snarled hair and not griping the hair above the comb. It's an awful ouch that can be avoided. Just pressing on the top of the hair shafts at the scalp helps.

If this seems a trivial entry it's because I've seen many mothers needlessly torturing their little girls by not using their heads for the sake of the child's head.

From what I see, jeans have become the national uniform. If all rear ends were uniform the fad wouldn't be so shockingly repugnant. What are the emotional hang-ups that push people into being carbon copies of everyone else?

63

For years I've pondered about my application of the Golden Rule when confronted with doing unto someone something I don't want done unto me. Please don't come visit me when I'm sick. I hate being seen when I look as lousy as I feel. To rustle up talk saps my germ fighting energy and flips my bugs up your nose. Just slip my food, drink and medication under the door and leave me alone either to die or get well.

However, I'll make a duty call to your bed ridden side, unless you're infectious, because I know you enjoy and expect callers. In other words, know you friends and their taste and do unto them what they want done, if it doesn't compromise you're principles.

Anyone ranting about raunchy and violent television programs being offensive is told, "Change the channel."

Changing the channel is the remedy? Ha! By the time I know I want to change the channel, I've already been offended.

?   ?   ?

When you think about it, the chicken should have come before the egg or the egg couldn't have been sat upon and warmed enough to hatch. Nor would the little embryo have had any idea of what it should eventually look like.

0   0   0

After all the years we were told eating eggs would damage our arteries, along comes news that chickens aren't out to kill us afterall. That a chicken can plan to lay a cholesterol free egg flys in the face of nature. However, if I were a chicken crammed in a wire bottomed cage out of which my feet poked, I'd not put anything good in my eggs either.

!   !   !

There can't be anything kind or loving connected to the philosophy of, "Let children learn by their mistakes." Why want them wasting time and money doing things wrongside out and upside down? Unrealitic, brutal and indicative of lazy parenting. Yes? Acceptable only if the child's prospective mistake is harmless.

What are restaurant owners thinking of when they advertise, "Home Cooking"? Don't they realize, if I want home cooked food, I'll stay home and cook?

Worse yet, some declare their home cooked meals to be as good as "mother made." If mother was a terrible cook, you wouldn't want to pay for any food remotely like hers. Perchance she was a gourmet chef and the fare you've just been served isn't anywhere near as tasty as hers, mother has been inadvertenly insulted.

A goofy sign on the drug store counter read, "Stay well, we want to see you every day."

For the store to turn a healthy profit, shouldn't it read, "Stay sick, and you'll need to see us everyday"?

The media often tells us more than we want or ought to know. It was dumb to announce that the first stall in all women's rest rooms is the least visited and therefore is the cleanest. Women, so informed, may begin visiting the first one almost exculsively, which then allows the second stall to make this claim. Ladies, figuring this out, head for the third. This could go on and on until no stall is any more tidy than the next.

Except to skin carrots, a vegetable peeler put to a potato wastes time; peels fly all over the kitchen; the spud must be turned around over and over again for the poker end to attack and dig out the eyes; the implement has a funny grip and crumples my knuckles.

Grandma's ancient paring knife fits my hand, cuts through large potatoes, noiks in and out of indentations with just a nudge. Contesting with a scraper lover, I knifed two potatoes to her one.

As with all the family furniture hand-me-downs I gladly accepted (cousins didn't and now regret it) dusting is a memory reunion. So it is using Grandma's knife, yet it really does get the job done faster and easier.

AS MY DINNER GUEST

Please arrive a smidgen before dinner time so my roast doesn't convert to leather and the rolls to bullets. The asparagus can't be started until you're visible because no hostess wants to serve green slime. If you're going to be late, you'd better have the best excuse in the world and you d better phone a good twenty minutes before you've become seconds late or you'll get tired lettuce, runny butter and one nervous, out of sorts hostess.

Please don't come bearing food, lest I think you think I can't cook or I suspect you think I'm so cheap you won't get enough to eat. Waldorf salad is on the menu, you tote in apple sauce and now there's too much of a good thing. And/or, if deciding to serve it, the table setting has to be rearranged and side dishes, that match the china of the day, need to appear instantly. A problem-they'll need washed.

I'll accept the sauce saying, "Thanks. We'll enjoy this tomorrow, dribble it into a bowl of my own, rinse and hand you yours when you leave----saving me a bowl delivering trip to your house another day and guilt if it isn't holding an edible.

See how an unsolicited contribution of food to a food affair can send the cook into orbit? Nor should you be bully about helping wash the dishes after being told, "No, I'll do them later." If anyone's going to break Grandmother's gold rimmed goblets, let it be me.

Complaints of not asking directions and leaving the toilet seat up are standard male traits that annoy women.

Other personality failures we can attribute to men: not stacking the trash--a small box inside a larger one, etc., so the half loaded wastebasket doesn't fill so fast. Doing so would reduce trips to the burn pile and keeps otherwise loose stuff from blowing into neighboring yards; never, never cleaning up the cruddy soap cake sprouting hair and congealed dirt splotches. Perhaps this is related to an innate urge to enshrine the bathtub ring as evidence of how hard they've worked-the dirtier, the more proof.

Also, wadding towels and shoving the knotted heap into the towel rack so it looks like a growth and can't breathe to dry; not sensing the importance of folding the outside towel edges to the inside and hanging it majestically straight with the backside no lower than the front. And, no interest in color coordinating towels, evidenced by a ragged, bilious green one mysteriously appearing and poked in among the original blue ones, not to mention it having been pulled from the bottom stack in the linen closet now in such disarray its door won't close; stand for ages in front of a drawer or cupboard looking for something, that shouldn't be there in the first place, and never move a single item on top or in front to see if the "thing" is under or behind; picking nose or ear without handkerchief and examining the residue.

Tell smart friends about your mind blocked foibles, when the occasion naturally arises or when you're out and out caught with a mental failing flapping. Confessing will endear you to their hearts. Admitting a harmless flaw, is an act of kindess giving them a momentary edge of superiority and the chance to supply you with a solution.

No one's been able to cure my two worst hangups and both take too much effort to hide. Not knowing the alphabet in small pieces makes looking up a word in the dictionary a real chore. What comes before or after " requires running through: "h, i, j, k, 1, m, n, o, p. Aha, there it is!"

Figures aren't my forte.(I still add 8 plus 6 on my fingers. My toes get in on 7 plus 9) . I detest time told as being 6:40. Twenty minutes to seven is instantly clear but 6:40 requires a muttering of "six thirty, thirty five, forty", while visualizing the clock's minute hand landing on eight. Ah, twenty mintues to, of, until, or before seven looms into my understanding.

By now it's 6:39 but, for Heaven's sake, say it's nineteen to or I'm on hold and bewildered again. Just mention numbers and prickly bumps gallop into my already rough blank spots.

See? Don't you now feel wonderfully intelligent?

For a carefree day, don't wear you watch and don't listen to or read any news.

I'm resisting owning a computer because: as a musician, I dislike the dull, lazy thunkings of the keyboard. The snap and crackle of my old typewriter keys keeps me dancing along and awake; the chance of receiving endless dribbles of E mail expecting reciprocal attention exhausts and overwhelms me just thinking about it; the screens are at a miserable height for biofocals; I'd resent wasting the time it takes pulling data out of the thing and arguing with it in the process; the fact that the Internet accepts pornography that can appear by surprise scares and revolts me.

How does a pro-choice pregnant woman defend having an abortion by believing, "It's my right, it's my body," when, with child, her body has become an "our" body?

CLOSING PRAYER: Father, help us to love enough to uplift and heal our land. Teach us how to unite families, rear our children in Thy precepts, cherish what is honorable in Thy sight, care for those in need. We pray for Thy guidance and forgiveness.

OFFERTORY

"Show us a home with young children and we'll show you a home where every pack if cards counts out at between 37 and 51.--Bill Vaughan

"Men show their character in nothing more clearly than by what they think laughable." -Goethe

"It now costs more to amuse a child than it once did to educate his father."-Herbert Prochnow

Gooey store bread cubes fail as Communion bread, in my estimation. They tend to clump together so when daintly reaching for one, you get seven. Brushing away six is a tacky, germy move, so, try shaking the six in the direction of the plate and hope they land somewhere within a polite vicinity thereof.

Once in your mouth, the store brand soon feels and tastes like an over-saturated spit ball. The wafer ones look like fish food, are flavorless and cling to the roof of your mouth.

To rescue the situation, ask the Communion Stewards if they'll like this recipe or allow you to bake and furnish the bread. The congregation will be grateful. It makes Communion even more special.

COMMUNION BREAD

4 cups flour
3 teaspoons baking powder
1 teaspoon salt
3 tablespoons butter, oleo or lard
1 cup sugar
2 cups milk

Bake in greased cake pans at 350 degrees about 45 minutes or until slightly brown on top and when testor toothpick comes out clean.
When cool, cut into cube sizes.
You can bake this in two loaf pans and then slice and cube.
Trim crusts if they're tough.

This bread freezes well so can be made ahead or, cubes not needed, saved for the next Communion.

Recipe of the late Johanna Carringer-Jamestown, Pa.

Concerning other foodstuffs, as they relate to church fund raisings: see if you can't coax servers into giving moderate size servings rather than immense ones that cut profits, create waste, smack of gluttony and offend those with normal appetites and capacity.

Assure those with hollow legs, they can have seconds if they find the first servings scanty. Better yet, have servers ask what amount someone wants. Handing out abnormally large portions has an aura of showing off more than merely being generous.

A different fund raiser is a jig saw puzzle afternoon or night. Charge admission, sell refreshments and have several tables prepared with puzzle pieces turned over and ready to go. Puzzlers are free to roam from one puzzle to another.

Try these. They can be whipped up in a jiffy and our grandchilren like making as well as eating them.

If you decide to crumble the crackers with your hands, remove your good ring(s) before hand. I lost a diamond in one batch the day the little ones were here and having a big time smashing the crackers. One of us must have swallowed the diamond because we searched every crook and cranny in the house and it didn't turn up.

Don't tell me, I know how I might have found it but elected not to sift through the business of everybody's business and perhaps still not find it.

CRACKER PANCAKES

Cracker pancakes are easy and quick to make. They're yummy, too. Mix the ingredients and fry as you would any pancake.

25 soda crackers   (place in a medium size bowl or pan.Using your clean hands, crumble the crackers into small pieces.)

Add:

1 egg(medium size.Or, two egg whites.)

1 cup milk (whole, 2% or skim)

Stir gently.The batter will be lumpy. Ladle onto greased griddle or skillet. Fry until golden brown and firm on on one side before turning. If batter begins to thicken,add more milk. This recipe makes eight (8) small,light and fluffy cakes.Serve with butter and maple syrup or honey.

Some day try broiled pears. Filled the crevices of canned pears with mayonnaise. Put in pan and pop under broiler until the mayonnaise turns golden brown. Serve hot with the meat course.

Desperate for a game to answer a child's, "What can I do now?, hand over a pencil and a list of the key words, without the answers.

INSIDE STORY

Rearrange the letters in each word to form a new word that relates to or helps describe each puzzle word.

Example: "Dinner" contains the word "Dine".

1. Chicken   (hen, chick)

2. Precipitation   (rain)

3. Vegetable   (beet)

4. Broadcasting   (airing, radio)

5. Domesticate   (tame)

6. Observe   (see)

7. Dismal   (sad)

8. Banister   (stair)

9. Transportation- a form of- (train)

10. Craft   (raft, art)

11. Devil   (evil, vile)

12. Health   (heal)

Remember, "I spy something that begins with---.", whatever letter starts the name of the object within view. A child unable to spell, plays the guessing game well by using colors in place of beginning letters.

Playing "mum" --"The first one to speak is a rotten potato"---interests pre-school children and gives relief for adults weary of their endless chatter.

I thought every grown-up in the world knew these games. I found I was wrong when enlisted to accompany a bus load of pre-schoolers on a half hour, sight seeing bus trip. The little natives grew restless and were soon hollering, tickling and poking one another. Singing songs lasted two minutes, total.

The four teachers couldn't, or didn't, come up with anything else to divert the wiggly, shrieking kids. Not ready to admit defeat, I went for "mum", explained how to play and was rewarded with 80 seconds of peace. Next, they picked up on, "I see something that's blue...?' After that ran its course, it was time to teach them the endless song with the lyric, "There's one foot, and there's two foot, and the other's name is foot, foot, foot. Three rabbits who play games/they have such funny names! there's one foot, and there's two foot and the other's name is foot, foot, foot. etc. etc.

Because I'd started the, "let's do this' routines, the teachers handed me my head, so to speak, for the return trip. Hard pressed to maintain the pace, I recalled the nonsense story: "I put a nickel in the gum slot to see the gum go down. You get the nickel and I get the gum because I put the nickel in the gum slot, see?"

After learning to speak this in sing-song rhythm, the trick is to repeat it starting every word with a letter sound used consistently:" Zi zut a zickel zin the zum zot,zoo zee the zum zo zown .... on and on. We got through a treatment with "dah" for "d" and "lah" for "1". The five year olds got the drift and ran with it. The smaller ones were content to listen to their classmates talking gibberish.

Short attention spans prevailed and we had another 20 minutes to fill. With my thinking cap running dry, I suggested we all play "four legged animal", each group counting how many four legged animals they could see from their side of the bus. It was a nice day and cows, a few horses and dogs were outdoors. I omitted the rule that has you bury all you've counted when you pass a cemetery. We didn't need tears dampening the last five miles. When pastures and yards gave way to busy streets and stop lights, "One by one, what did you like best about what you saw today?", got us home sane and sound.

What astonished me was all the teachers saying they'd never heard of "mum" or "four legged animal". This struck a stab of terror in my heart wondering how many other young teachers and care-takers missed hearing these sillies in their childhood? Rudimentary as such attention getters are, compared to walking, talking toys and video games, they have a calming effect. Anything that calms has esthetic value just as a dose of unadulterated nonsense has a way of keeping us playful, sharp and well rounded.

For good measure, I showed the teachers how to play, "Knock on the door, peek in, lift up the latch and walk in.' Gently, one first taps on the <u>child's</u> forehead (the door line), raise the eyelid by pushing up, gently still, on the part of the eye right below the eyebrow (peek in), lift the tip of the nose, doubling as the latch and pretend to walk your fingers into the child's mouth to illustrate the last line. Toddlers enjoy this.

I hope "Here's the church, here's the steeple" hasn't been completely retired. I trust the five little pigs won't ever get lost on their way to market. "Ring around" and London Bridge" have play limitations for grandparents whose bones don't jangle painlessly any longer.

Even though the littlest talking people don't quite get the point of the knock, knock jokes, puns and other play on word funnies, run them out anyway. It a bit like being forced, in school, to study a subject you swear you'll never need knowing about. In spite of believing the time to be total loss, unbeknowst to you, it's teaching your mind to work.

A tired, baby sitting grandmother lamented," I don't know why I volunteer to spend so much time with these tots. I doubt they'll even remember me after I'm dead."

She admitted that being with them pepped her up as much as it wore her out. Whereupon, I assured her she was teaching feelings they'd never, ever forget. How priceless and vital to their eventual well being.

So it is with instilling the capacity for humor although the children may not understand much of what it's about when it first goes past them.

A money saving formula is waiting three weeks before buying something you think you want.

For over-wanters, it's probable that at the end of three weeks some other desired item has replaced the first. In another three weeks, the second has been ousted by a third.

As three week segments continue, wants keep changing with no money spent. This is a super plan for teen-agers, to which I can attest; mother instituted the 21 day wait to teach me thrift. Our sons practiced it. It doesn't do much for the national business economy but does wonders for one's private finances and keeps the house from overflowing with useless stuff.

$*   *$

An idea for ball cap makers to get guys to wear the hats frontwards would be to create a line with a visor-bill on the front AND the back. This way they could alter the look by wearing the hats sideways to shade BOTH shoulders. To eliminate bills altogether would save the company money.

Working a crossword puzzle with a pen requires a special kind of arrogant confidence.

Two friends, able to hold the answers in their heads before applying the ink, astound us puzzlers needing pencils with fat erasers that soon become pencils with only a pimple of rubber showing. (Eraser cleaning tip: for the ones that get hard and black and royally smudge up the paper, rub the daylights out of them on the carpet or a hunk of sandpaper and they'll go you three more puzzles.)

For what it's worth: using a razor blade or decent knife, cut a pink pencil eraser into tiny rounds. Makes cold cuts for your dollhouse kitchen.

+

A stunt: have a person go three steps up the stairs and stop. The stunt doer now gets behind the climber and grabs both the climber's ankles. As the climber starts up the stairs, the ankle holder, following the climber up each step, adds hand-arm strength, slightly upward, simultaneously with the climber's leg liftings.

The climber experiences the sensation of almost flying by losing some control of his movement upward. It's great fun for the one ascending, hard work for the lifter helper. Don't let little kids try this without supervision.

Whatever the generation, youngsters enjoy silliness. "Oh! Susanna", with the lyric of, "It rained all day the night I left, the weather it was dry". .is funny fun. So is the tune, "The Capital Ship". Remember that one? "A capital ship for an ocean trip is a walloping window blind." It goes on to introduce the "cinnamon bats" wearing "water-proof hats" and the "cook was Dutch, and behaved as such, for the diet he gave the crew-ew-ew, was a number of tons of hotcross buns served up with sugar and glue."

Planning this to be sung for a children's program, a helper vowed today's child wouldn't enjoy it. It got in anyway and the kids giggled themselves breathless. A kid is a kid in any old time bracket. Don't be duped into thinking what amused you and your children years ago won't tickle the "modern" child.

This trick gets a rise out of young and old. Complicated to explain, so read carefully.

Put the palm of your right hand up against the palm of someone else's left hand. Next, make a open fingered "C" with the middle finger and thumb of your free hand. Now place your thumb on the outside, lower part of your middle finger that's against the other player's palm. This places your thumb against the outside back of the other player's middle finger. The object is to now stroke upward from the bottoms of both middle fingers--yours and the other Person's--keeping the "C" shape but closed over the middle fingers of both hands.

Stroke up a couple of times until you feel the sensation of not knowing which middle finger is yours or the other person's. It creates a numbness, dead-like feeling that's quite weird.

It's a hoot!

Nearly every child able to sing knows "Jingle Bells". With several children on hand, four's about the minimum, give each an animal name for which a voice sound can be mimicked. One will be a "oink" pig, one a "quack" duck, another a moo cow, the last a "barking" dog.

Explain that during the singing of the song, when you point to one child, he/she will enter singing with the animal sound instead of the usual words. When you point to another child, the former singing animal stops.

Second time around--all are to sing their part at the same time still in place of the tune's words. It's a circus.

Toddlers to six year olds find the "Steinway Scream" attention getting. Works with a grand piano, no matter the brand. Requires two adults and one or more kiddos.

Sit on the bench with a child on your lap, the others beside you and additional kids standing nearby. Have the second adult, or a youngster loving to yell, go to the back end of the piano.

You put down the damper pedal and hold it down. Have the screamer lean in over the lower end of the piano strings and shout, "Hello" or someone s name-- whatever. Single words behave best. Have eveyone agreeing to be quiet and once the word is flung across the opened strings, an eerie echo results. Re-engage the pedal with each new word.

While you've got them corralled, push back the music rack and strike notes in the middle range of the keyboard. They'll enjoy seeing the hammers bobbing up and down and you can snatch a moment's sitting time.

Here's the church

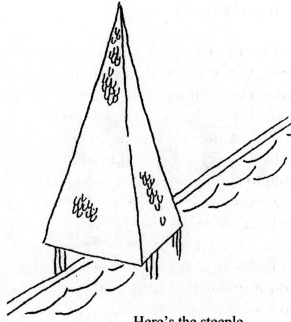

Here's the steeple

Here's the choir

Where are the poeple

Here's the church

Here's the steeple

Where's the choir

Here are the people.

Honestly, near sighted people really do hear better with their glasses on. It's amazing how much good listening depends on watching moving lips.

      0—0   0—0

The skunk smells? No, the skunk stinks, we smell. Okay, so technically the skunk has a nose and is able to smell. To explain: when the skunk sprays we don't say he's' putting up a smell, we say he's putting up a stink.

       =   =   =

Hey, claiming to be warm blooded because cold doesn't make you shiver is backwards; it's because you're cold blooded, like frogs and fish.

      u   c

Writing teachers aren't teaching good, tight writing when they assign a 1,000 word essay on a subject that could be covered in 500 words or less. In fact, a student should earn a higher grade for turning in a theme that's short, sweet and to the point.

Requesting a long report as punishment also punishes the teacher, who has to read and correct it.

Because each younger generation wants to scare the pants off and thoroughly disgust the older ones, they're obligated to behave in worse fashion than did the last bunch.

This happening, along with the older generations growing more rushed, tired and spineless, is one reason society keeps going downhill. So much for the prediction, "One day soon, the pendulum will swing back.'

So, what's stopping it? Is it stuck? Let's hope we figure out how to jump start the thing! Perhaps we ought not to entertain hope, after contemplating what Nietzsche concluded: "Hope is the worst of all evils, because it prolongs man's torments."

Not to be entirely glum, I suppose life's blueprint of every positive having its negative keeps us humble. It also keeps us trying and going along like that battery Bunny .Will Rogers said," Even if you're on the right track, you'll get run over if you just sit there." So keep on hopping.

Have you noticed that frequently life's goods and bads frequently add up to zero? It's only when minus zero refuses to be nudged into the black that we've got a problem.

To sum up, "You keep on getting what you've been getting when you keep on doing what you've been doing. "A tidy quip with no name attached.

No credit either for this summing up of the sum up: "Enjoy the little things, for one day you may look back and discover they were the big things."

POSTLUDE

Old age is like a sentence being erased one word at a time: "Good glory, nothing much goes along working well."; "Good glory, nothing much goes along working."; Good glory, nothing much goes along. Good glory, nothing much goes."; Good glory, nothing much)'; Good glory, nothing."; Good glory."; Good." (Norma Leary)

"Nobody grows old by merely living a number of years People grow old by deserting their ideals." (Normal Instructor and Primary Plans)

"Old age is like everything else. To make a success of it you've got to start young." (Felix Marten)

"Denunciation of the young is a necessary part of the hygiene of older people, and greatly assists in the circulation of their blood."(Logan Pearsail Smith)

Author's comment Mightn't it also improve the younger people's hygiene and circulation?

Thanks to Adam and Eve having messed up the Master plan big time, the Golden years can be more tarnished than shiny. Be armed in advance by listening to the complaints of oldsters, the most of whom will advocate the special genius needing cultivated to stand upright, avoid day long backaches and keep your underwear clean. Also, to execute movements and jobs that once were accomplished easily by a body willing to cooperate.

Not only is the term 'Golden' annoying, so is "senior citizen." Being a senior implies impending graduation, if the senior makes the grade and passes.

Since 'passing' is the almost exclusive buzz word for 'dying', you can readily see how being called a 'senior' revs up horrible thought progressions.

As one accumulates years, it's reasonable to accept the prospect of death knowing, finally, that hanging onto the table and refusing to go isn't going to be fruitful. The worst fear is the possibility of losing one's mind. However, if one's body has melted down beyond repair, maybe being unaware of it would be a blessing if pain could be banished.

When a body becomes worn out and contrary, it's necessary to outwit it. Making half the bed and scrubbing away half the bathtub ring before your get out of each, is a beginning. Learning to go to the bathroom before it becomes pressing to do so,is wise. By waiting,an aging bladder tends to get your motor going faster than your wheels. Just approaching the toilet on the run accelerates this process and God help you if your panties get twisted, stuck or don't fall down in jiffy-quick order.

Lest I forget, it's expedient to learn your telephone ringings, as compared to those sounding through your television set. I wonder how many people have gone to their great reward prematurely as a result of racing and falling to answer their nonphones?

Arthritis takes its toll and also has an ambiguous element: the more you move the less joints are frozen; to move more requires larger meals to fuel the energy needed to stir about; larger meals add body weight to further stress joints and/or makes the eater sleepy. Nodding off stops mobility and in turn re-creaks the stiffening ball and socket parts. Amassing extra calories, half of which an older body refuses to assimilate nicely, due to a now sluggish, rebellious disgestive system, sets up the misery of bloating accompanied by a series of noises you didn't know you were capable of producing.

Drinking more water, so as not to turn into a human puffball, makes sense until you realize doing so sends you to the bathroom and gobbles up more time than you wish to spare. Because, either great patience is taken to sit until all is clear or the messy crotch problem becomes a trial.

I tell you truly, by the time you're in your seventies, you'd better have a strategy in mind to offset these upcoming difficulties and stave off worrying your adult children as long as possible. They're already wondering what the devil they're going to do with you when you completely fall apart. In the meantime, abiding your stale breath, concrete toenails, thinning hair, wrinkles that look like an expert seamstress smocked your skin, and listening to you telling the same story five times in five hours, gives them enough to hurdle before round the clock nursing enters the picture. What a crock knowing you may become a financial and embarrassing burden to them and yourself, as you dissolve into a heap without even trying.

The only way to remotely endure aging gracefully, rather than disgracefully, is to search for more about it that's funny than tragic. That's a tough exercise unless you have friends with active funny bones and in the selfsame state of disrepair. Still, you daren't dwell long on recitations of ailments for fear you sympathetically imagine additional ones you'll do better without.

Hearing that old age presents a challenge is true. Hearing that it takes a great deal of courage is also true. There are some advantages, such as getting a discount on your restaurant bill. Eating out is a bit of a two edged sword deal if you have dentures. Half the food doesn't chew well with slow teeth and there's no way, in public, you can zip out your partial to remove the particles beneath it that are jabbing you unmercifully.

What do you do when certain people frequently give you surprise gifts and later come to shop in your store? I feel like an ungrateful wretch if I don't outright give them an inexpensive item or a discount on a costly one, although I didn't ask for what they gave me and often didn't want or need it either. Not accepting their offerings is also rude so I'm really in a spot, as is my store's profit margin and livelihood. It's also unfair to other store owners and customers if I don't charge the going price. Giving Sally a discount or freebie of more value than what she originally gave me and away we go again in both directions.

Much as I try to keep business dealings from personal ones, I'm still bothered by the situation made more sticky when I'm given a gift Tuesday and the giver comes shopping Thursday. Have I been bribed? Am I cheap if I don't return the favor and, if I do, have I started the entire process all over again?

This is different than my wonderful neighbor lady advising not to keep track of givings and receivings but, instead, let both go down whatever random path pops into view.

You know, when I'm bone tired and lack the steam to write thank you notes, it's then I wish people weren't so nice to me.

For better care and sympathy, go to a doctor with the same ailments you have. Find out, too, the name of your doctor's doctor in case your's is away when you have a flare up. Your doctor's doctor must be a fine one or your doctor wouldn't doctor with that doctor. (It's been fun doctoring this doctor squib.)

Do you suppose men, generally, get better medical attention than women because men's body parts are larger? Does bass clef moaning command more attention than a woman's treble squeaks and chirps?

When boys, did male doctors see their mothers unable to be sick so the household wouldn't fall apart and hence deducted that women rise so well above pain and agony there's no sense in taking their complaints seriously?

Might it be because men are less verbal and enjoy a challenge more than women? Thus, men not reciting symptoms as detailed and colorfully sets the male doctor to prying and feeling, gleefully, like a detective?

There must be reasons why my Jim gets 40 minutes of concentrated attention, a prescription, pat on the back and ten smiles for a mere sticky eyewinker. With my feet about to fall off, I get two minutes, no medication and three frowns indicating my feet are in my head. "So, help me with my head," doesn't get a nod either.

Five months later, my feet go back together probably because my run-down, work-about shoes finally fell apart. My present backache, probably brought on by the tilted footwear, will doubtless be exchanged for neck pain resulting from babying my back and walking on an angle. Perhaps a hardy sinus infection will take my mind off my neck until the heels of my new work shoes run lop-sided and the foot business begins anew. In the meantime, I shan't bother the doctor unless the sinus trouble multiplies. Then the trouble will truly be in my head.

On June 11, 1997, Dan Rather reported and confirmed what women have known for centuries: "Women get four times LESS medical care than men."

Since women live longer than men, this seems to suggest that we're better off getting less testing, attention and medication. Let the guys work on one another and we girls will keep the house and world going amid aches, pains and sinus headaches and our moaning men.

Perchance we must succumb to seeing the doctor, let's lower our voices(if we opt to speak at all),sit high and straight and stare into space with a slight expression of defiance. With this attitude dancing around the examining room, the doctor will be puzzled and diligent. After all, if we're not talking there must be something seriously wrong. Give him the opportunity to dope out a diagnosis and conquer death single handedly, albeit it temporarily. Should such a charrade prove tiring, women need a female doctor.

Postpone your cataract surgery until after Christmas.

This is so you may enjoy how one or two fogged lenses enlarge, fuzz and blend holiday lights into an etheral delight.

Before cataracts have you missing the last stair step that jolts your frame apart, it's restful not seeing dust on furniture, cobwebs in corners, fingerprints or fly specks.

x　　　*x*　　　*x*　　　*x*

On days my knees don't bend and I march down stairs stiff-legged (a trick needing learned years ahead of time), I wish someone had told me, when I was a kid, that we've been allotted only so many comfortable bends. In that case, I'd have saved some.

*　　　*　　　*

Men don't like lolling about in robe and slippers as much as do women--at least not in my family. Jim equates bumming around, robe bound, a surefire sign of laziness. He fails to see how much faster I race through early morning housework unencumbered by slipping, binding, motion-hampering underwear.

He hasn't a clue as to how a bra, strong enough to keep a female front from sagging to the navel area, or beyond, reduces one's breathing ability. How panties and panty hose can choke a crotch and waistline. How all these combined items dig deep, red ruts into a woman's thinner skin.

He's never worn a woman's shoe with sole so thin that steeping on a bread crumb can hurt. Would that he should experience reaching to a high shelf or hanging wallpaper and having a strap skate to his elbow to render him dangerously arm-locked at a crucial moment.

Not that I hold my underwear in contempt. Quite the contrary; it's vital in keeping my body parts together. And, I can't, imagine running madcap through my housework naked, as I've heard some maverick minded do. I'd be immediately cold and get skin puckers in unmentionable places.

=　　　=　　　=

Of Grandparent age but having no grandchildren, one would benefit from borrowing a young child for a few hours each week.

Grandchildren are the best bonus of age and I wish I'd had ours before I was a parent. Meaning, I'm a better grandparent than I was a parent. It figures because neither am I as busy in the same ways as when a young adult.

All this withstanding, elders being around children have an excuse to play again, to marvel at the wonders of nature. Grandparents are beyond the hustling years that gobbled time spent with jobs, committees and raising the children you made smart enough to bear grandchildren. Now they do the chasing amid jobs and committee meetings. (Part of this is a repeat. I'll not apologize for being of the age to repeat myself about a topic dear to older hearts.)

We need these youngsters as much as they need us: five year olds can program a VCR; set the microwave or car radio clock; open the childproof medicine bottle before we die within the two hours it takes us to wrestle it open.

Creative, dedicated care of grandchildren dupe our grown kids into thinking we were better parents than we actually were. Grandchildren are always glad to see us and don't care if we repeat ourselves. If their dog also likes us, our children are the more convinced we're of noble fiber.

There's nothing better to get rusty bones, brains and hearts moving than having a grandchild spend time with you.

Assuming you've sense enough not to ask about what you've sense enough not to want to know about aging, it is sensible for anyone under 50 to believe the complaints of their elders. It teaches one to appreciate not having reasons for such gripes--yet.

Old age doesn't move in as gradually as you might think. After a normal Tuesday, I awoke Wednesday with my laugh lines hysterically deeper and further shoved askew by a disgusting, pleated cheek groove from eyebrow to chin. The stiff neck wasn't jolly either. To avoid such a sight and crick, refrain from sleeping on your stomach and never have a dressing table light brighter than 40 watts.

The shock of facing my distorted visage was not softened by deciding to trim my toenails and finding they'd turned to concrete, literally overnight. If soaking in a hot tub doesn't melt them adequately for regular scissors or clippers to hack, locate a pair of industrial strength nail clippers. The local veterinarian might be a source. Wire cutters might do...a hacksaw is the last option. I'm kidding about the hacksaw.

Not having time to iron wrinkles and pillow treads, I needed to upgrade my face before hurrying to the store. I grabbed some clear adhesive tape and smushed an end into the left jaw jowl, having gravitated to a new low since Tuesday night. Nor did the right side one look all that upstanding either.

Next, tugging the attached tape in a northerly direction, I fastened the other end into my hairline, in front of my ear. Pleased with the uplift rubbing away twenty years, my smile popped the jaw tape end off. I began again. Pulling the gooey end out of my sideburns region was a misery.

I started fresh and hit upon the idea of winding the top tape ends around my glasses' bows. This was tough and caught gobs more hair into the tape tops but it elevated assorted jowls to nostril height. I resisted smiling.

On the way to the store, my ear tops and head began aching in earnest. Unable to find an "on sale" heater, the clerk called the manager, explaining, "There's a little old lady up here wanting to know. .

"Little OLD lady?" Lordy, I'd just taped away half a century and I'd never, to date, heard "old" applied to little ole me. It hurt. It was a shock!

In haste, I looked about for whomever else might be older and in search of a heater. Not another "old" in sight. I was devastated.

The manager came bearing the sought-after heater. Thrilled, I made the grave error of grinning broadly. One tape, anchored starboard, crinkled loose. The manager, seeing this Humpty Dumpty act, must have thought I was having a stroke. "Are you all right, Madame?" he asked.

Here-to-fore I never been called Madame. What a lousy day. As hilarious and insulting this day's unfoldings, I eased the worried fellow by confessing failure to hoist my waddles. I also yanked my glasses off and snatched away all remaining tape. Presto! The ear and headache vanished and all face sides matched.

Still smarting with all the "old" references, I vowed that was my last do-it-yourself face lift. Before this, I'd tried the commercial lift things with the band through the hair and glue on the tape ends. The glue produced a rash and the band flattened hair where hair needs to be.

This fiasco episode prepared me for how future encounters may unfurl now that I'm the picture of "old":. I needn't show my birth certificate before the senior citizen discount is subtracted from my bill; nurses will ask what medications (plural) I'm taking, figuring there are several; no life insurance salesmen will stop, "seeing" what a bad risk I am.

Shortly after the clerk voiced my oldness, so did one of several letters arriving from school students, whose teacher had previously brought them to our house on an abbreviated field trip.

They were attentive hearing about and looking at the miniatures, playing the tone chimes, listening to the organ, watching Jim demonstrate the letter press, show various pieces of printing paraphernalia, hand setting type to print out their names.

We host several of these tours yearly and the teachers always prod the kids into writing thank you notes--good training and appreciated enough to keep us continuing our show and tell episodes.

The letter below is indicative of the general tone of all the notes, but the last line of this one was special:.

"Thanks for letting us come over to see all of your dollhouse figures. They were small. I could never the patience to do that. The organ was my favorite thing to see. It had a lot of buttons I wouldn't understand. Mr Leary's workshop machine was an old piece. Most everything was old and in good shape there."

Jim and I were highly amused realizing that this young man was probably including us among everything old. If so, being in good shape was comforting.

Wearing white hair and wrinkles" proudly", because we've "earned them", may be touted as a badge of honor but it does little to cheer me. Mightn't the fading and crinkling be a bodily announcement that we weren't smart enough to escape or triumph over the heaps of horribles before they took their toll? I feel a personal deficiency when I'm sick. Not rational since time and germs are built into the system and to "take a licking and come up ticking" is the plight of living. The humbling therein is a necessary evil without which we'd drown in our accumulated pride.

There are a few ways to handle wrinkles: wear long sleeves when the arm flesh resembles thin elephant hide with a harlequin design; when sitting at a table, visiting with friends over tea, lean on your elbows and place flat of each hand on each side of jaw and gently push fingers upward; keep smiling constantly--it deepens the laugh lines but puffs out the creases in the cheeks. Lastly, don't lean way over an infant's face when changing its diaper. To illustrate what a shock this can be to a tiny person, put a mirror flat on a table and then hang your face down over it. You too, will be frightened and revolted by the falling, wiggling, bunching folds that look all the world like a balloon that's just lost all its air.

Given the physical adversities of diminished eyesight and missing teeth, don't look into a mirror at bedtime.

To be a grandmother, you first have to be a mother-in-law, you hope. Mothers-in-law are the butt of all those bad jokes that are grossly unfair if their daughters-in-law are impossible louts. On the side of balance, the world needs daughter-in-law jokes.

Mother-in-law jokes are a spoof,
When a mom-in-law has the proof
To back up her claim,
That the one causing blame
Is a miserable pain and a goof!

(Blessedly, not in my case. I have one of the best.)

Betcha' the reason Grandmothers and Grandfathers are moved to tears more easily than before grandchildren arrived is because they have a deeper well of time and emotion from which to draw upon.

The mellowing of older folks may very well come from being tired. Also, having learned that pesky problems aren't all that world shaking and yes, the sun will come up again tomorrow.

The duo makes two reasons why grandparents spoil their grandchildren-it's easier to give in than to argue. "Good" spoiling is giving what little ones need--time, attention and love that just can't quit.

So what if that extra cookie spoils his dinner?

When good table manners were a sign of good breeding, we kids were told, "Don't leave your sail up", meaning when finished eating pudding or soup, the spoon was to be put to rest on the service plate and not left in the dish, cup, etc.

The rule was observed so the person removing dishes wouldn't hit the spoon and send food and dish every which way.

In these times of fewer underplates, the sail up has to happen. It's still obtuse but not as bad as a diner plunking a butter-laden, food sogged utensil smack down upon the table cloth! To my dismay, I had someone do this during a rather formal dinner we were hosting. The silverware misplacer hadn't been," born in a barn", as we used to accuses anyone not knowing or minding their manners. The "not knowing" are to be forgiven but what one does about the "disobeyers", I haven't a clue. I guess it's race to soak the cloth as soon as dinner's over.

Any waitress telling me, "Keep your fork", after I've ordered dessert, breaks my heart.

"No, I'd rather not. Please, bring me a clean one," I implore, as sweetly as I know how.

Lordy, I don't keep my fork for dessert at home so I'm not about to start when out for a dinner I'm paying enough for to deserve and kindly be given one.

To reduce stress we're advised to ignore the jingling telephone, crying baby, whistling tea kettle, barking dog and whatever else is beckoning that's bothersome. Unless you have a secretary, nurse, chef and animal trainer to dispatch to quiet these things, letting them ring, cry, whistle and bark only adds stress to stress.

We're to stop hurrying to be on tine. Being late stresses both the waiter and the later. Rushing to get the lawn done before it rains makes sense; the rain's going to nurse the half you've mowed to new heights and the half you haven't fnished yet to higher heights. Get going at the sight of the first dark cloud.

Get as far away as possible from people dedicated to stressing you habitually unless you love them and kicking them out would give you more stress than they cause.

Let's get real and admit that without stress we'd get little done, our bodies would decay from inactivity and our brain power blink off. There 's nothing like a deadline to get a body out of bed and to work. So, we get the jitters once in awhile. It's better than sitting around in neutral. And then there's oops, gotta go, the toilet's running.

Answering machines are enigmatic--as hateful as they are helpful. Connecting with one, when cost is involved, is paying for a call that isn't. When a quick return call is vital, there's the worry that the machine's playback isn't working. If it is, will the person truly return the call since there's seldom time after a beep, or seven annoying ones, to state reasons why a call back is badly needed?

Not knowing whether you get the machine because the owner's in the bathtub or away for three days, raises pesky questions: cancel errands and stay home awaiting the return call; dial back every hour hoping to finally hear a live voice?; ring the person's neighbors to have them run a safety check? The neighbor notion fizzles when you get their recording; NOW what? Resume your life, turn your machine on and know that answering machines answering answering machines could go on for days. Sorta' like receiving a thank you note for your thank you note.

The advantage of reaching a long distance answering machine is sticking the returnee with the toll for a good long conversation the second time around.

Machine intros of blathering comedy routines waste my time and nickel. Bless those confirming the number reached. Nice not to confuse a stranger. Although, if they're curious and phone you back, perhaps you'd strike up a friendship.

Once upon couples walking together, the man put himself between the street side and the woman. He did so to protect her from road damage: puddle splashes; flying horse manure bits; air-borne stones; any missile rising from the antics of an erratic driver. Naturally, this walking ritual originated when streets were dirt, males inherently guarded females and females appreciated the gallantry, including no raunchy talk in their presence.

By the time I was strolling with fellows, mud roads were past history. The guys of the 40's honored this walking nicety nicely, shifting gracefully into place in the transition of changing directions-turning a corner or turning around.

This rite of passage has gone by the boards (not a reference to board sidewalks). Seldom do I see couples, except those of my era, observing this congenial custom nor do I see many young, adoring men opening car doors, store doors or house doors for their adorable young women. Humph! Another amenity sluffed off, partly because of the libbers leaping to prove how capable they are.

"I can do it myself," Libby bristles, yanking the door half off its hinges and stoving her shoulder's rotary cuff.

In summary, gals shunning a guy's polites insults his mother's training to shape his basic and base proclivities into that of a refined gentleman. It's also silly not to capitalize on his superior, muscle power.

I'm for all the "hims" in my life intercepting projectiles aimed my way, toting the heaviest bundles, mowing the lawn, pumping gasoline and anything else that boosts their male ego. Helping my husband and three sons feel inportant makes me more important and rested.

±   ±   ±

The first time I saw Kotex on a store shelf without its brown wrapper disguise, I nearly swooned. Imagine my horror when television sprouted ads for feminine hygiene spray, douches, bras and, lastly, condoms. Note, the inequity here.

Why not ads for jock straps, deodorant dip?

I can't imagine how men ever ride a horse or bicycle in comfort. What a chore of rearranging this must entail, considering how I must wiggle when wanting to sleep painlessly on my stomach. Horses and bikes hit bumps.

Dr. Freud? There are plenty of ladies without a inch of penis envy. Convenient as it might be to urinate standing up or fun to write one's name in the snow, moving with a top has to be easier than running about with a smaller equivalent between one's legs. Alas, I'll never know, will I?

Jock strap ads could include cup sizes. Wasn't that a hoot about the girl Little Leaguer being told she should wear one of those cup gadgets? Different fabrics could be touted along with washing temperatures and non-allergenic soaps to give the dainty contraption beauty and long life. Maybe a model with garters or suspenders to eliminate ride up or ride down--something we women could use when clad in those skimpy panties with a string crotch and leg holes yawning open to the waist. Talk about being sawed in two. Worse, I can't, on the first try, get into the dratted things; the wispy crotch is the same size as the leg openings.

Shaving to accomodate the "vee" look of women's swim wear is akin to being "preped" for childbirth. I haven't the itch resistance for that scene. I don't like the elongated look anyway.

Worse is the bare behind with thong. Speak of being cheeky! Is there no shame?

Bathing beauty movie star Esther Williams founded a swim suit company years ago. She admired the one piece suit that made a woman's body sleekly curvaceous. Apparently she isn't taken with the latest swim fashions. She's credited with describing the suits of today as being nothing but "two cups and a string."

The therapeutic principle of keeping a journal in which to vent your anger may indeed keep you law abiding, divorce free and your offspring giving you a tolerable amount of respect.

Keep it where no one will find it. Discipline yourself to never re-read prior entries. They might revive your original fury and augment it. Tell a dear, trusted friend where it's kept and appoint the friend to burn it immediately after your death. This arrangement includes the friend swearing never to read a word of it no matter how tempted.

On second thought, destroy the vitriolic parts today. Heaven forbid, you could go there before you get the proper precautions in place. Don't gamble with having memories of you tarnished by leaving a legacy of mean spirited notes.

Complaining in a diary is akin to writing a nasty letter you never send to one you'd like to poke in the nose. If it's a letter you find necessary to mail, let it sit two days while you cool off. Reword the thing if its tone is so ugly it's bound to breed return contempt rather than reform.

Maybe you'll find it needs to be meaner yet and sent to the company or person you'd like out of your life forever. Omit anything that might spell a future law suit.

Unable to halt the ravages of the antiquating meltdown skid I'm in, I often scan crowds hoping to see others more scrawny, greyer, thinner, wrinkled and more badly turned out than I. In this era of dress having gone from casual to casuality, the latter is easy and uplifts without aid of a Wonder Bra.

In the process of comparative body spying, I get side tracked first by dodging, in terror, the overweights lumbering toward me. Secondly, young, firm bodies togged out in rag bag outfits, seemingly contesting for the, "Dump Frump", title, are a depressing distraction.

A black tent tends to slim blubber blobs that refuse to budge off and goodness knows the thinnies need long sleeves and long pants to hide Minnie Mouse toothpick limbs as well as falsie fronts.

Will the young, nicely stacked person please explain the lure of wearing non-fitting clothes? Those without gussets, tucks, darts, gores, belts, and are three sizes too large in the non-bargain?

More often than just being color blind, these ugly print garment buyers aren't bothered by long, meandering hemlines tickling ankles an inch above grubby sneakers or combat-type boots with ankle socks lopping out. These shapeless dresses aren't actually worn--they merely hang as if from invisible nails somewhere in the shoulder region.

Having lived through the eye-insulting garb of the hippies, the double knit and mini skirt rage, what the heck is this and why do we need it? Enough, yet.

Not up on the latest craze terminology, I screwed up my courage and asked son, Nate, and daughter-in-law, Becky.

"Do girls, boys too, have any name for looking like something dragged through a knothole backwards? Tell me what you know about the 'look' that makes me sorry I did! In my opinion, it stinks."

"And you're opinion, if aired around, will come off as grumpy and stuffy," opined Nate, without hesitation.

"But I am grumpy and stuffy and probably, more truthfully, repelled and pained. In case you don't know, this fad of lousy appearance is a self-defeating one."

"Be careful not to condemn all teen—agers," warned Nate. "There aren't that many running around looking, on purpose, like poverty stricken grandmothers of a century ago."

"That's what you think. Two are too many and I saw five last week at the Mall."

"Our baby sitter says the new style as been around awhile and is known as the, "Grunge", look, " offered Becky, getting to the point by supplying the definition that says it all.

"I do agree that black lipstick and blue fingernails give the impression that one has died and just been dug up," admitted Nate, a conservative dresser. "This cadaver war paint doesn't photograph well either." Nate's a photographer and hence finds most of his customers attempting to put their best face forward. Hence, he believes I'm having delusions about seeing so many shabby young people out and about.

"Are you going to mention frizzy hair?, Becky wants to know.

"Certainly. I just wish there were more words to describe unkempt. What do you think of the confused follicle bedizened bedlam syndrome?"

"Bedizened?" Nate inquired, none to softly.

Becky to the rescue. "I dont' see as many frizzle head freaks as before. Maybe that hair is on the way out."

"I hope so because they look like they're glued on a bushel of shredded, corrugated cardboard. Scraggy and uncombable. Isn't it odd that those with naturally curly hair labor to smooth it and the smooth haired strive for curls? My generation would have wept copiously had our hair looked so grizzly."

"Give it up, mother." Nate was beginning to sound exasperated. He often gets that way with me although he loves to argue and sometimes learns something from an harangue. We once spent a year on whether or not farmers were dumb. I'd been one for a few childhood years and knew, as a group, they weren't dumb at all. I finally convinced him farmers were students of life rather than tall building experts. This done, Nate was allowed to keep his room here until he finished high school, provided I was always to have the last word.

He went on. "As long as you're going to skewer everyone and everything you find displeasing, and especially if you decide to write about some, go overboard so you don't come off as little minded and prehistoric. Best to hammer out tongue-~

93

in-cheek exaggerations. Sound less preachy," Nate said.

"You've been reading Lewis Grizzard again, haven't you? I'm not Lewis and furthermore he's dead and beyond the reach of being sued. I'm not sure what you mean anyway."

"Well, like auto drivers. Hit on the typical ones with greasy hair, oil spotted jeans, moth-eaten sideburns."

''That's mean.

"Not any meaner than your assumption that messy, smelly people live in houses reeking of cat urine and dying house plants."

"I might have said something like that about that guy with the slippery, shiny brown suit offset by black shoes and white socks. However, I didn't write about him. Anyway, it was just a guess," I defended. "The fellow's complexion was dim and clogged. I'll bet he doesn't eat right. I'll wager he doesn't have money for clothes either. Therefore, he's to be forgiven. Although, " I prattled on," I'd think he could try soap or a sand scrub from a near-by stream."

Jim ambles in and reminds us all of zoot and leisure suits and his own high school gang's penchant for wearing Derby hats." You girls wore snoods and head scarfs. Turbans too. And, those sky-scrapper high pompadours were murder."

"Shush! You're not helping my cause. I'm only griping from the days of 'protest to grotesque', when I first became repulsed and can't hope to recover unless I rant."

"Good luck, Norm," Becky added in a comforting, nonsarcastic tone.

Nate changed the topic of discussion by asking if we could keep kids while he and Becky ran off for needed two day break?

He knows my first priority is loving grandchildren and he knows I think I take better care of them than any young parent can be expected to do, partly because I evision death in everyone's every move and youngsters move more than all of us put together.

Yes, we'd be glad to have the children for the weekend. We'll be two weary grandparents come Sunday night but just imagine how many gems of wisdom we'll blather by them between playing catch and paring back the crayon stub wrappers.

For 48 hours, Jim and I can pretend to be kids again and stop long enough to watch an ant lugging a crumb twice as big as he is, dig in the garden, chase a firefly and renew the amazing, thrilling reality of the blessings grandchildren are and the abundance of those they so readily embrace and pull us back into.

Now for grandchildren and gift giving: The latest and more honest approach to gifting is NOT to buy something you yourself would want.

Our older grandgirls covet clothes and since I'm stuck in another dress time slot, it's expedient to give them cold, albeit, impersonal cash. Doing so means I spend more than I might by finding some old fashioned, tailored, sporty, solid color, good fitting thing on sale.

But on sale things can't always be exchanged and even if it weren't a sale thing, I could be worn to a frazz hunting up the sales slips and traipsing about making the exchanges, none of which would suit them the second time around either.

I'm pleased to report that our teenage granddaughters do clean up nicely and look like females. As you might ascertain, I've swished my oar about in their wake of fashion tastes urging what little alignment with mine I can foster, shy of vowing to otherwise disinherit them.

The girls did drive home one frighting possibility of why it's smart to look bedraggled instead of alluring.

"You want us to be safe, Gram", explained Meg. "So, it depends on where we're going what we wear."

"You go places where you mightn't be safe?" I was frantic.

"Not on purpose but you can't be sure what type of unsavories might cross your path these days."

No one, not even Nate, can disagree that this state of affairs is pitiful.

In summary, I must hasten to say that even the ratty clad are more desirous to see than the, "show-everything except-nipples- and- crotch" crew. Acres of bare, quivering flesh is the worst. Nor does it photograph well!

The above segues into the consensus that people don't get dressed up as often as they once did and why they ought to take the plunge more often.

People all togged out in their "Sunday go to meetin' clothes", uusually sit straighter to keep from wrinkling their finery, eat more carefully to avoid stains, walk lightly so as not to scuff their shoes and zooch mud onto their stockings or pant legs.

Decked out, one is more prone to keep fingers out of eyes, nose and hair. So as not to smudge makeup and crumble a coiffure.

The climax is talking and listening more intelligently in an effort to live up to the smart looking clothes.

CODA

"On the whole, I think we shall survive. The outlook is as bad as it has ever been, but thinking people realize that--and therein likes the hope of its getting better."
Jawaharlal Nehru

Together maybe we could get the Ten Commandments back on public walls. With sin and guilt playing dead, doing what feels good is taking center stage. As Dr. Laura advocates, "Don't put up with wrong to be liked."

Because few people would dare to spank a Grandmother, we, of the old fashioned set, can get away with making very pointed remarks on behalf of our beliefs that worked.

Don't let anyone get away with saying, "Oh, in your day there was just as much wrong, you just didn't hear about it." That's not so. Not that my heyday era was wholly pristine and unblemished, only that parents, friends and teachers won't put up with disrespect, bad attitudes and laziness for a second. Unless you wanted to be shamed, stigmatized, and chance being out and out ostracized, you straightened up.

Agreed that we hear more horror stories than in days past. The media hammers us relentlessly with every awful happening. They're not just reporting news, often they're creating it because good news is boring. Who wants to hear that the airplane left on time, arrived on time and there were no problems?

A little tyke once told me, "One good turn deserves a push." The moment's at hand to push for more good turns. There are still enough good turn people to turn things around if not afraid to call a spade a spade. Silence is approval.

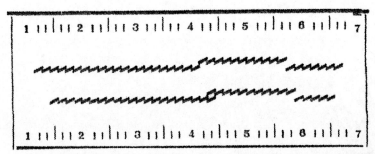

Q. Of which composer does the above remind you?
A. Bach.

Q. *A* centipede organist?
A. No. Pipe organ ciphers

Q. A rhythm band score?
A. Wrong again. A monotone alto.

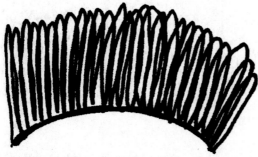

Q. An Indian headdress?
A. Organ pedals as seen by a nearsighted organist who broke her glasses.

Q. Give up?
A. A 'hymnotized' organist after **six long verses.**

ABOUT THE AUTHOR

Norma Leary is a free lance writer living in Jamestown, Pa. She was formerly a photo-journalist and her work has appeared in numerous magazines. She taught piano for 40 years, was organist-choir director in Jamestown for 41 years and currently is the organist for two churches in Conneaut Lake, Pa. She also owns and operates a Dollhouse-Miniatures Shop in Jamestown.

Her husband, James, is a retired printer and book binder. "After three weeks of formal retirement, Jim set up a print shop in our basement," Norma reports.

Jim and Norma have three grown sons and six grandchildren, all of whom they see frequently. "We're lucky to have everyone within squeezing distance," Norma cheers.